ENCOUNTERS
WITH THE
ARCHDRUID

BY JOHN MCPHEE

John McPhee
ENCOUNTERS
WITH THE
ARCHDRUID

Farrar, Straus and Giroux

New York

Seventeenth printing, 1988

The text of this book originally appeared
in *The New Yorker*, and was developed with the
editorial counsel of William Shawn and Robert Bingham.

Published simultaneously in Canada
Printed in the United States of America
Designed by Betty Crumley

To Robert Bingham

Contents

▲

PART 1

A Mountain

A small cabin stands in the Glacier Peak Wilderness, about a hundred yards off a trail that crosses the Cascade Range. In midsummer, the cabin looked strange in the forest. It was only twelve feet square, but it rose fully two stories and then had a high and steeply peaked roof. From the ridge of the roof, moreover, a ten-foot pole stuck straight up. Tied to the top of the pole was a shovel. To hikers shedding their backpacks at the door of the cabin on a cold summer evening—as five of us did—it was somewhat unnerving to look up and think of people walking around in snow perhaps thirty-five feet above, hunting for that shovel, then digging their way down to the threshold. Men from the Chelan County Snow Survey use the cabin in winter while they

3

measure snow depths and snow densities, and figure how much runoff to expect at the time of thaw. Because of the almost unbelievable amount of snow that can accumulate in that part of the State of Washington, what they do there is a vital matter to the people below and even far beyond the mountains.

What we were doing there was something else again. We were tired. We had walked seven and a half miles uphill since three that afternoon. One of us was in his sixties, another in his fifties, and all of us saw the cabin as a haven from what obviously would have been very cold ground. Until midsummer, the trails had been impassable, and to make the trip we had had to wait for the winter snows to melt. An entry in the register in the cabin said that snow had fallen one week earlier, August 5th. But we had been drawn to the Cascades in part because a great many people believed that they were the most beautiful mountains in the United States. A somewhat smaller and, on the whole, more parochial group felt that these huge, conical peaks, raised in volcanic fire and later carved by moving ice, were the most beautiful mountains in the world. In 1964, the United States Congress set aside this region and others as permanent wilderness, not to receive even the use given a national park, not to be entered by a machine of any kind except in extreme emergency, not to be developed or altered or lumbered—forevermore. Within the structure of this so-called Wilderness Act, however, was a provision known as "the mining exception": all established claims would remain open to mining, and new claims could be made in any wilderness until 1984. At the foot of Glacier Peak, in the center of this particular wilderness, is a copper lode that is half a mile from side to side. The Kennecott Copper Corporation has a patented claim on this deposit and could work it any time. We wanted to have a look at the region while it was still pristine. The others left it to me to add their names to the register in the cabin: Charles Park, geologist, mineral engineer, who believes that if copper were to be found under the White House, the White House should be moved; David Brower, who has been described by Stewart Udall as "the most effective single person on the cutting edge of conservation in this country," leader of a conservation organization called Friends of the Earth; and Larry Snow and Lance Brigham, medical students from the University of Washington, who were along to help with the logistics of the trip and perhaps incidentally to give first aid.

A mouse ran out from under the cabin, made a fast move among the packs, and went back under the cabin. We collected firewood and water. There was a cascade, white and plummeting, beyond the cabin. We changed into warmer clothes and lighter shoes. Brower, who hiked in twill shorts and a T-shirt and soft gray Italian boots, put on a long plaid shirt, trousers, and a pair of basketball shoes. Although he was out of shape, Brower was a prepossessing figure. He was a tall man. He had heavy bones, thick wrists, strong ankles. And he had a delicate, handsome, ruddy face, its features all finely proportioned but slightly too small, too refined, for the size of his frame, suggesting delicacy. His voice was quiet and persuasively mellifluous. He had an en-

5

gaging smile and flashing white teeth. He was in his late fifties, and he had a windy shock of white hair. Brower had dropped out of college when he was nineteen, and disappeared into the Sierra Nevada. He had spent his life defending mountain ranges and what, by extension, they symbolized to him, and one of the ironies of his life was that his love of the mountains had long since drawn him away from them and into buildings impertinently called skyscrapers, into congressional corridors, into temporary offices in hotel rooms, into battle after battle, and out of shape. (In the idiom of conservation, "battle" is the foremost term for what conservationists do, and conservationist publications are "battle tracts.") Brower's skin was pink from the work of the climb, and when he was taking off his soaked T-shirt he had revealed a fold across his middle. The mouse ran out again from under the cabin, looked around, its nose vibrating, and retreated.

Lance Brigham said, "Stick your head out once more, mouse, and it's curtains for you."

Brower said softly, "It's we who are the intruders."

Park had been taking off his boots—made in Canada, of heavy leather—and was putting on a pair of sandals. He grinned cryptically. He, too, had a shock of white hair. He was in his sixties, and he was as trim and hard as a college athlete, which he had once been, and nothing about him suggested that he had ever been out of breath. From his youth to the present, he had spent a high proportion of his life in the out-of-doors, and a high proportion of that in wilderness. Going up the trail that afternoon, with his geologist's pick in his hand, he whacked or chipped at half the boulders and rock faces we passed, and every once in a while, apparently for the sheer hell of it, he rapped the pick's hammer end on the stump of a tree that had been taken to clear the trail.

"That's a habit I developed long ago—banging on rocks and stumps," he said.

"Why?"

"Kodiak bears. I never wanted to take one by surprise. The same is true in Africa of leopards and gorillas. In other words, never take an animal by surprise."

Park spoke slowly, not because he was hesitant but simply in a measure that seemed compatible with geologic time. He had an almond face, alert gray eyes, and a mobile smile that tended to concentrate in one or the other corner of his mouth. He was even taller than Brower, and he wore khaki from head to foot. He had a visored khaki cap.

Not far into the mountains from their eastern extremity, at Lake Chelan, we had come to an oddly formal landmark. It was a sign that said, "You Are Now Entering the Glacier Peak Wilderness Area." In other words, "Take one more step and, by decree, you will enter a preserved and separate world, you will pass from civilization into wilderness." Wilderness was now that definable, that demonstrable, and could be entered in the sense that one enters a room.

Park said, "Will they let me carry my pick in there?"

"Until 1984," said Brower.

We stepped across the line. I said, "If we get lost in here with that pick, we may discover a new copper deposit."

Brower said, "If you make a new discovery, I'm here to see that you don't get out."

We moved on into the wilderness. The trail was dusty. It was covered with a light-brown powder too fine to be called sand. Park said it was glacial flour—finely ground rock coming out of the ice, ice of the past and ice of the present. Far above us in the high cirques were glaciers—the Lyman Glacier, Isella Glacier, Mary Green Glacier, and, perhaps prophetically, the Company Glacier on Bonanza Peak. The sky was blue and cloudless, a day to remember in the Cascades. Brower said he was disappointed that it was not raining. He explained that he did not like dry duff but preferred the feel and the beauty of a wet and glistening forest, vaporous and dripping. He said that he hoped we would be fortunate enough to have a good rain before the trip was over. He labored slowly up the trail, taking it conservatively, eating thimbleberries and huckleberries as he moved along.

"There are no really old rocks in the Cascades," Park said, nicking a rock in passing. He picked up and admiringly turned in his hand a piece of pistachio-green epidote. Two hundred yards up the trail, he rapped at an outcropping with his pick and said, "That is volcanic." Minutes later, he swung again, sent chips flying, and said, "That is contact rock." This in some way entertained Brower, who laughed and shook his head. I remembered once driving through the Black Hills with Park, and how he would stop his car from time to time and just sit there looking at rocks. As a boy in Delaware, Park used to collect rocks and think about the

8

West. While he was still in Wilmington High School, he had fifty ore minerals in his collection—hematite, malachite, galena, chromite. "I wanted to study mining, not particularly geology—mining," he said. "I just wanted to get into rocks. Mining has always appealed to me. It's in the out-of-the-way places."

A serrated ridge several miles from the trail had a reddish glow in the late-afternoon light. "See that color? That's pyrite," Park said, pointing. "Copper often comes with it. If I were in here looking for copper, that's where I'd head." The copper terrain we wanted to see was still more than ten miles away, however, and we stayed on the trail.

We passed a big Douglas fir, at least six feet in diameter, that had crashed to earth in the recent past, and Brower said how nice it was to see it there, to know that some lumber company had never had a chance at it, to see the decay stage of a natural cycle—the forest reclaiming its own. If dead trees are not left to rot, he said, the ecology of the wilderness is disturbed. Park kept his reactions to himself. His eye wandered to a square hole in a cedar stump. He waved his pick in the direction of the stump and said, "Pileated woodpecker." We moved on.

After a series of switchbacks had lifted us seven hundred feet in less than a quarter of a mile, we stopped to rest by a stream that was alternately falling through the air and racing down the mountainside. Everywhere, from every slope, the Cascades cascade. Water shoots out of cracks in the rock, it falls over the edges of cliffs, it foams, sprays, runs, and plunges pure and cold. Enough snow and rain fall up

9

there to irrigate Libya, and when water is not actually falling from the sky the sun is melting it from alpine ice. Down the dark-green mountainsides go streamers of white water, and above the timber-line water shines against the rock. In every depression is a tarn, and we had passed a particularly beautiful one a little earlier and, from the escarpment, were looking back at it now. It was called Hart Lake and was fed by a stream that, in turn, fell away from a high and deafening cataract. The stream was interrupted by a series of beaver ponds. All around these free-form pools were stands of alder, aspen, Engelmann's spruce; and in the surrounding mountains, just under the summits, were glaciers and fields of snow. Brower, who is an aesthetician by trade and likes to point to beautiful things, had nothing to say at that moment. Neither did Park. I was remembering the words of a friend of mine in the National Park Service, who had once said to me, "The Glacier Peak Wilderness is probably the most beautiful piece of country we've got. Mining copper there would be like hitting a pretty girl in the face with a shovel. It would be like strip-mining the Garden of Eden."

Park wiped his forehead with his hat. I dipped a cup into the stream and offered him a drink. He hesitated. "Well, why not?" he said, at last. He took the cup and he drank, put the cup down with a smile, wiped his lips, and said, "That's good stuff."

"It's melted glacier ice, isn't it?"

Park nodded, and swallowed a little more.

Brower drank from a cup that was almost identical to mine—stainless steel, with low, sloping sides, a wide flat bottom, a looped wire handle—with the difference that in raised letters on the bottom of Brower's cup were the words "Sierra Club." Brower for seventeen years had been the executive director of the Sierra Club—its leader, its principal strategist, its preëminent fang. In the mountains, a Sierra Club mountaineer eats and drinks everything out of his Sierra Club cup, and in various wildernesses with Brower I had never seen him eat or drink from anything else. In the past, in the High Sierra, he had on occasion rubbed pennyroyal-mint leaves over the embossed letters in the bottom of his cup and added snow and whiskey for a kind of high-altitude julep, but he rarely drinks much in the mountains and there was no whiskey at all on this trip. That night at the snow cabin, we ate our dinner from our cups—noodles, beef, chocolate pudding—and hung our packs on high rafters and were asleep before nine. We slept on bunks that had been tiered in the improbable cabin. At two in the morning, we were all awake, with flashlight beams crisscrossing from various heights in the compact blackness.

"What the hell is going on?"

"What is it?"

"What's there?"

"Four very beautiful little tan-and-white meadow mice," Brower said.

"Aw, for heaven's sake," Park said, and he went back to sleep.

Park, throughout his career, had not made a religion of camping out, and he had been particularly pleased when we found the cabin and its bunks, although they were little more than stiffly woven wire in frames. His general practice on trips of exploration for minerals had been to sleep in a bed if there was one within five miles, so he had managed to keep his lifetime total down to something like nineteen hundred nights on the ground. On foot and alone, he had hunted for copper in the Philippines, in Cuba, in Mexico, in Arizona, in Tennessee. He had hunted for silver in Nevada and Greece, for gold in Alaska, gold in South Dakota, and—on one curious assignment for the United States Geological Survey—gold in Alabama, Georgia, South Carolina, North Carolina, Virginia, and the District of Columbia. He had found what he was looking for. During the Second World War, there was a working gold mine in Rock Creek Park, in Washington, D.C. Such is Park's feeling for where ore bodies are that some of his friends think he has occult powers. For fifteen years or so, he used his skills in the name of the Geological Survey. Then, in the late nineteen-forties, he began to teach geology and mineral engineering at Stanford University, where he eventually became Dean of the School of Earth Sciences. From one base or the other—Washington or Palo Alto—he has never stopped hunting the earth for metal, sometimes as a consultant to various companies. He has looked almost everywhere for iron and manganese. He once set up a base camp at fifteen thousand feet in the Chilean-Bolivian Andes and, working up from there, found iron at seventeen thousand feet. In 1956, he was taken in a pirogue up the Ivindo River, in Gabon, to a point from which he took compass bearings and walked for two weeks through jungle. On relatively high ground, elephant trails were so wide and hard they were like roads, but in swamps the elephants' footprints were like postholes. The canopy was so thick it obscured the sky. Park had had serious back trouble for some time, and one day he fell to the ground and could not get up. He lay there for two hours until something jelled, and he got slowly to his feet again and moved on. He was hunting for iron, and he found a part of what is now called the Belinga Deposit. Even in the United States, he usually stayed out, alone, for about two weeks at a time. He went light, eating out of his frying pan and drinking from a small tin cup. He has used the same pick for twenty years. He speaks of the rootlessness of the life of an exploration geologist and says that many people tend to be discouraged by it. "You're just wandering. You're on the loose." He has planted gardens spring after spring and never seen his plants in bloom. Instead, he has drawn from the earth its mercury, lead, zinc, uranium, fluorspar, phosphate, nickel, molybdenum, manganese, iron, lithium, tin, copper, silver, and gold.

In the morning, soon after we were again on the trail, we went around the north edge of a lake that had a surface of at least ninety acres and was almost as big as the glacier that was dripping into it from fourteen hundred feet above. The effect of glacial flour in still water is to turn it green. As we moved uphill, and looked back, we saw that there were three other green lakes, closer to the glacier. In them, small icebergs were drifting. Ahead of us, and far above, was a ridge that ran north-south and dipped at one point to form a shallow notch. This was our immediate destination, and it had been named Cloudy Pass, because the most distant view a person usually has there is of his own groping hands. On this day, though, the sky was without clouds anywhere. The climb was steep toward the pass and we tended to string out. Brower, in the lead, said again that he wished it were raining.

I asked him if, by his own standards, he would describe the terrain we were in as wilderness. "Yes, it is wilderness," he said. "The Sierra is what I love, but these mountains are perhaps the most beautiful we have." Then he accelerated his pace and was soon far ahead. He seemed to be feeling good, getting into rhythm with the mountains.

A mosquito bit Park on the wrist, and he slapped it. "They follow the snow," he said. "The higher we get, the more mosquitoes there are."

We climbed on in silence for a while, and then he asked why Brower had gone on so far ahead.

"I don't know. He seems to want to be alone," I said.

"He certainly is—let's say—reserved," Park said. "I don't see how anyone could ever break through it. I almost called him yesterday when he said the big trees ought to be left to rot in the forest. Long before they fall, they are dying from the inside out. It's a shame not to use big trees like that." He waved his pick at a stand of spruce. "I am not a member of the Sierra Club," he went on. "I don't approve of their policy. To me, they are preservationists, not conservationists. You can't avoid change. You can direct it, but you can't avoid it. I like Sierra Club books, though."

In 1960, in Yosemite Valley, Brower helped put together

14

an exhibit of landscape photographs and accompanying swatches of prose. Then he developed the idea of circulating the exhibit in book form. The result was the Sierra Club's Exhibit-Format series—big, four-pound, creamily beautiful, living-room-furniture books that argue the cause of conservation in terms, photographically, of exquisite details from the natural world and, textually, of essences of writers like Thoreau and Muir. Brower was editor and publisher. He selected the photographs. He wrote the prefaces. In this way, as in others, he brought the words "Sierra Club" into the national frame of reference. He published Exhibit-Format books on everything from the Maine islands (*Summer Island—Penobscot Country*) to the Grand Canyon (*Time and the River Flowing*), the region of his own youth (*Gentle Wilderness—the Sierra Nevada*), and the mountains we were now crossing (*The Wild Cascades*). Within nine years, people had paid ten million dollars for Exhibit-Format books, and Brower said he had been surprised to find that people were willing to pay that much for beauty. Brower himself was certainly willing to spend money on it. Once, a set of picture proofs did not look quite right to him and he had ten thousand dollars' worth of plates thrown out. Udall gave *Time and the River Flowing* to Lyndon and Lady Bird Johnson for Christmas, 1964. At twenty-five dollars a copy, the books were, in a sense, investments, and rich conservationists bought them in round lots. Struggling conservationists could buy them in compacted form as three-dollar-and-ninety-five-cent paperbacks.

With Brower as its executive director, the Sierra Club

grew from an organization of seven thousand members to an organization of seventy-seven thousand members. The figure seems both large and small. There are more people in Cedar Rapids than there are in the Sierra Club. Nonetheless, under Brower the club became a truly potent force, affecting legislation that had to do with the use of the land, the sea, and the atmosphere. Brower was not the leader in every battle. He concentrated on certain foes, and many were in the Department of the Interior. To the Bureau of Reclamation, he is the Antichrist. They say there that Brower singlehanded prevented the construction of two major dams in the Grand Canyon for at least two generations and possibly for all time. On the Green River in Utah, Brower stopped cold a dam that would have inundated parts of Dinosaur National Monument. In the cause of mountains, he and lieutenants in the State of Washington fought loggers, miners, and hunters, and won a North Cascades National Park. For nearly twenty years, Brower has crossed and recrossed the United States campaigning for conservation before every kind of audience. The federal government's Outdoor Recreation Resources Review was his idea. He was a primary force in the advancement of the Wilderness Act. His counterparts in other conservation organizations long ago acknowledged him as "*the* spokesman for protected wilderness." Once, when Brower had driven for several hours through wretched fog and rain to attend a meeting and make a speech in Poughkeepsie, I asked him if he could say why he did all this, and he said, "I don't know. It beats the hell out of me. I'm trying to save some forests, some wilderness. I'm trying to do anything I can to get man

16

back into balance with the environment. He's way out—way out of balance. The land won't last, and we won't."

Having moved above the trees into a clear area, Park stopped to look back over the forest, the green lakes, the glacier, the snowfields, and the white peaks beyond. I asked him if, from his experience, he would call this wilderness. "No," he said. "Not with this trail in it." He agreed that what we were looking at was almost incomparable, and he said he doubted if Brower saw anything he didn't see. "That is a beautiful view," he went on. "And these are magnificent mountains. They remind me of the Chilean Andes. But how is a mining company operating a pit on the other side of this ridge going to hurt all this? I don't see it. My idea of conservation is maximum use. I think preserving wilderness as wilderness is a terrible mistake. This area is one of the few places in the country where copper exists now in commercial quantities, and we just have to have copper. The way things are set up, we can't do without it. To lock this place up as wilderness could imperil the whole park system, because in ten years or so, when copper becomes really short, people will start yelling and revisions will have to be made. Any act of Congress can be repealed." Park was speaking slowly, and we were making our way up through open alpine meadows that were splayed with streams and full of heather, lupine, horsemint, daisies, and wild licorice. "I'm in favor of multiple use of land," he continued. "Have you ever been in the Harz Mountains? With proper housekeeping, you can have a mine and a sawmill and a primitive area all close together. When the Kerr-McGee Corporation wanted to mine phosphate on the coast of Georgia, conservationists

17

howled. A hearing was held, and twenty-six people, most of them representing groups, testified against Kerr-McGee. *No one* testified for them. This shocked me. It was like people standing around watching a man get beat up. When Texas Gulf Sulphur drilled three holes and found an ore body in Ontario, people accused them of hiding information. I testified before the S.E.C. on their behalf. The image of copper companies is bad today, with all this conservation poop. There's a Clark's nutcracker!" The nutcracker, in flight, was a hundred feet above us.

We were now about to top the final rise to Cloudy Pass, where Brower was waiting. We looked back again over the eastward view—lakes, peaks, beaver ponds, cascades, snow, ice, white-ribbon streams, and dark-green forests. Again Park said, "I don't see it. I don't see how a mine on the other side of this ridge is going to affect that." Park lives in a trim, attractive, solid-looking one-level house on a dead-end street in Palo Alto, and beside his front door is a decorative grouping of green rocks—copper ore—and an old pick with a broken handle. With his present pick, he swung at an outcropping with what seemed to me to be unusual curiosity and force.

"What are you looking for?" I said.

A grin came into the corner of his mouth. "Nothing," he said. "I just haven't hit one in a long time."

▲

Most of the pass was covered with snow, but there were some patches of bare ground, and these were blue, green, red, yellow, and white with wild flowers. The air felt and smelled like the first warm, thaw-bringing day in spring in Vermont, and, despite the calendar, spring was now the season at that altitude in the North Cascades, and summer and fall would come and go in the few weeks remaining before the first big snow of September. Brower had dropped his pack and was sitting on a small knoll among the flowers. Park and I and Brigham and Snow dropped our own packs, and felt the sudden coolness of air reaching the sweatlines where the packs had been—and the inebriate lightness that comes, after a long climb, when the backpack is suddenly gone. The ground Brower was sitting on was ten or fifteen feet higher than the ground on which we stood, and as we went up to join him our eyes at last moved above the ridge-line, and for the first time we could see beyond it. What we saw made us all stop.

One of the medical students said, "Wow!"

I said slowly, the words just involuntarily falling out, "My God, look at that."

Across a deep gulf of air, and nearly a mile higher than the ground on which we stood, eleven miles away by line of sight, was Glacier Peak—palpable, immediate, immense. In the direction we were looking, we could see perhaps two hundred square miles of land, and the big mountain dominated that scene in the way that the Jungfrau dominates the

19

Bernese Alps. Glacier Peak had originally been a great symmetrical cone, and that was still its basic shape, but it had been monumentally scarred, from within and without. It once exploded. Pieces of it landed in what is now Idaho, and other pieces landed in what is now Oregon. The ice sheet mauled it. Rivers from its own glaciers cut grooves in it. But it had remained, in silhouette, a classic mountain, its lines sweeping up beyond its high shoulder—called Disappointment Peak—and converging acutely at the summit. The entire upper third of the mountain was white. And below the snow and ice, black-green virgin forest continued all the way down to the curving valley of the Suiattle River, a drop of eight thousand feet from the peak. Spread around the summit like huge, improbable petals were nine glaciers —the Cool Glacier, the Scimitar Glacier, the Dusty Glacier, the Chocolate Glacier—and from each of these a white line of water ran down through the timber and into the Suiattle. To our right, on the near side of the valley, another mountain—Plummer Mountain—rose up about two-thirds as high, and above its timberline its snowless faces of rock were, in the sunlight, as red as rust. Around and beyond Glacier Peak, the summits of other mountains, random and receding, led the eye away to the rough horizon and back to Glacier Peak.

Brower said, without emphasis, "That is what is known in my trade as a scenic climax."

Near the southern base of Plummer Mountain and in the deep valley between Plummer Mountain and Glacier Peak —that is, in the central foreground of the view that we were looking at from Cloudy Pass—was the lode of copper that

Kennecott would mine, and to do so the company would make an open pit at least two thousand four hundred feet from rim to rim.

Park said, "A hole in the ground will not materially hurt this scenery."

Brower stood up. "None of the experts on scenic resources will agree with you," he said. "This is one of the few remaining great wildernesses in the lower forty-eight. Copper is not a transcendent value here."

"Without copper, we'd be in a pretty sorry situation."

"If that deposit didn't exist, we'd get by without it."

"I would prefer the mountain as it is, but the copper is there."

"If we're down to where we have to take copper from places this beautiful, we're down pretty far."

"Minerals are where you find them. The quantities are finite. It's criminal to waste minerals when the standard of living of your people depends upon them. A mine cannot move. It is fixed by nature. So it has to take precedence over any other use. If there were a copper deposit in Yellowstone Park, I'd recommend mining it. Proper use of minerals is essential. You have to go get them where they are. Our standard of living is based on this."

"For a fifty-year cycle, yes. But for the long term, no. We have to drop our standard of living, so that people a thousand years from now can have any standard of living at all."

A breeze coming off the nearby acres of snow felt cool but not chilling in the sunshine, and rumpled the white hair of the two men.

"I am not for penalizing people today for the sake of future generations," Park said.

"I really am," said Brower. "That's where we differ."

"Yes, that's where we disagree. In 1910, the Brazilian government said they were going to preserve the iron ore in Minas Gerais, because the earth would run short of it in the future. People—thousands and thousands of people in Minas Gerais—were actually starving, and they were living over one of the richest ore deposits in the world, a fifteen-billion-ton reserve. They're mining it now, and people there are prospering. But in the past it was poor consolation to people who were going hungry to say that in the future it was going to be better. You have to use these things when you have them. You have to know where they are, and use them. People, in the future, will go for the copper here."

"The kids who are in Congress in the future should make that decision, and if it's theirs to make I don't think they'll go for the copper here," Brower said.

"Sure they will. They'll have to, if people are going to expect to have telephones, electric lights, airplanes, television sets, radios, central heating, air-conditioning, automobiles. And you *know* people will want these things. I didn't invent them. I just know where the copper is."

Brower swung his pack up onto his back. "Pretend the copper deposit down there doesn't exist," he said. "Then what would you do? What are you going to do when it's gone?"

"You're trying to make everything wilderness," Park said.

"No, I'm not. I'm trying to keep at least two per cent of the terrain as wilderness."

"Two per cent is a lot."

"Two per cent is under pavement."

"Basically, our difference is that I feel we can't stop all this—we must direct it. You feel we must stop it."

"I feel we should go back, recycle, do things over again, and do better, even if it costs more. We mine things and don't use them again. We coat the surface of the earth—with beer cans and chemicals, asphalt and old television sets."

"We *are* recycling copper, but we don't have enough."

"When we knock buildings down, we don't take the copper out. Every building that comes down could be a copper mine. But we don't take the copper out. We go after fresh metal. We destroy that mountain."

"How can you ruin a mountain like Glacier Peak?" Park lifted his pick toward the mountain. "You *can't* ruin it," he went on, waving the pick. "Look at the Swiss mountains. Who could ruin *them?* A mine would not hurt this country —not with proper housekeeping."

Brower started on down the trail. We retrieved our packs and caught up with him. About five hundred feet below us and a mile ahead was another pass—Suiattle Pass—and to reach it we had to go down into a big ravine and up the other side. There were long silences, measured by the sound of boots on the trail. From time to time, the pick rang out against a rock.

Brower said, "Would America have to go without much to leave its finest wilderness unspoiled?"

We traversed a couple of switchbacks and approached the bottom of the ravine. Then Park said, "Where they are more

23

easily accessible, deposits have been found and are being—or have been—mined."

We had seen such a mine near Lake Chelan, in the eastern part of the mountains. The Howe Sound Mining Company established an underground copper mine there in 1938, built a village and called it Holden. The Holden mine was abandoned in 1957. We had hiked past its remains on our way to the wilderness area. Against a backdrop of snowy peaks, two flat-topped hills of earth detritus broke the landscape. One was the dump where all the rock had been put that was removed before the miners reached the ore body. The other consisted of tailings—crushed rock that had been through the Holden mill and had yielded copper. What remained of the mill itself was a macabre skeleton of bent, twisted, rusted beams. Wooden buildings and sheds were rotting and gradually collapsing. The area was bestrewn with huge flakes of corrugated iron, rusted rails, rusted ore carts, old barrels. Although there was no way for an automobile to get to Holden except by barge up Lake Chelan and then on a dirt road to the village, we saw there a high pile of gutted and rusted automobiles, which themselves had originally been rock in the earth and, in the end, in Holden, were crumbling slowly back into the ground.

Park hit a ledge with the pick. We were moving up the other side of the ravine now. The going was steep, and the pace slowed. Brower said, "We saw that at Holden."

I counted twenty-two steps watching the backs of Brower's legs, above the red tops of gray socks. He was moving slower than I would have. I was close behind him. His legs,

24

blue-veined, seemed less pink than they had the day before. They were sturdy but not athletically shapely. Brower used to put food caches in various places in the High Sierra and go from one to another for weeks at a time. He weighed two hundred and twelve pounds now, and he must have wished he were one-eighty.

Park said, "Holden is the sort of place that gave mining a bad name. This has been happening in the West for the past hundred years, but it doesn't have to happen. Poor housekeeping is poor housekeeping wherever you find it. I don't care if it's a mine or a kitchen. Traditionally, when mining companies finished in a place they just walked off. Responsible groups are not going to do that anymore. They're not going to leave trash; they're not going to deface the countryside. Think of that junk! If I had enough money, I'd come up here and clean it up."

I thought how neat Park's house, his lawn, and his gardens are—his roses, his lemon tree, his two hundred varieties of cactus. The name of the street he lives on is Arcadia Place. Park is a member of the Cactus and Succulent Society of America. He hit a fallen tree with the hammer end.

"It's one god-awful mess," Brower said.

"That old mill could be cleaned up," Park said. "Grass could be planted on the dump and the tailings."

Suiattle Pass was now less than a quarter mile ahead of us. I thought of Brower, as a child, on his first trip to the Sierra Nevada. His father drove him there from Berkeley in a 1916 Maxwell. On the western slopes, they saw both the aftermath and the actual operations of hydraulic mining for gold. Men with hoses eight inches in diameter directed water with such force against the hillsides that large parts of the hills themselves fell away as slurry.

"Holden was abandoned in 1957, and no plants of any kind have caught on the dump and the tailings," Brower said.

Holden, in its twenty years of metal production, brought out of the earth ten million tons of rock—enough to make a hundred thousand tons of copper, enough to wire Kansas City.

Park said, "You could put a little fertilizer on—something to get it started."

When we reached the pass, we stood for a moment and looked again at Glacier Peak and, far below us, the curving white line of the Suiattle. Park said, "When you create a mine, there are two things you can't avoid: a hole in the ground and a dump for waste rock. Those are two things you can't avoid."

Brower said, "Except by not doing it at all."

▲

In a bottle gentian, Brower found a butterfly drinking. With a quick but precise move of his hand, he picked it up. He said it was a monarch and that it had a flying range of two thousand miles. "Monarchs almost have a sense of humor," he went on. "They play with the wind." He let the butterfly go, and it went up into the wind, looped, dipped, and sailed off on an oblique tack through voids of air against the backdrop of the big mountain. Noting patterns, habits, frequency of wingbeat, Brower can identify butterflies in flight. He will be moving along a trail and his eyes will be attracted by flutterings sometimes hundreds of yards away, and he will say, for example, "Parnassian." I was with him once near Piute Pass, in the Sierra, when he saw a Parnassian beating its way west, and he said he was impressed by its being at that altitude, which was twelve thousand feet. On the same day, he found a California tortoiseshell butterfly—orange, black, and yellow—sitting on a rock. He picked it up. It was so cold it couldn't move. Brower warmed it up, and it flew from his hand.

There is a butterfly called *Anthocaris sara reakirtii broweri*. Brower discovered it, when he was fifteen years old. He was a solitary boy, a collector of butterflies, and he knew he had something unusual when he saw that its primaries were black and white and the undersides of its secondaries were green. He found it near Grizzly Peak, in the Berkeley Hills, where he used to go for long walks after school as a boy, sometimes leading his mother by the hand. She was blind, and he would describe to her the terrain they were moving through and the plants and animals he saw. His mother was a tall, attractive woman. She had an advanced degree in English literature. An inoperable brain tumor had blinded her when he was eight.

Brower was born in Berkeley, in 1912. When he was a year old, his mother went shopping one day at a Red Front store and left him for a few minutes in a baby carriage on the sidewalk. Squirming around, he fell to the pavement, and smashed out several of his front teeth, damaging also the wall of the gums. His second set of front teeth did not come in until he was twelve, and when they did they were awry. He was ashamed, embarrassed, unsure of himself, shy. He was afraid to smile. In school, he was known as the Toothless Boob. He withdrew into the Berkeley Hills—which are now covered with houses, including his own house, but were wild then. He also liked to go to Two Rock Valley, some fifty miles north of Berkeley, to the chicken ranch where his mother had grown up. The place was a haven for both of them. Brower avers that he could hear the chickens growing there. He also says he learned to talk with chickens. He believes that tones cross the barriers of species. There was a mare at Two Rock Valley that no one could handle, but whenever Brower went near her she whinnied cordially and did as she was told.

Brower's father taught mechanical drawing at the University of California. He was a small man (five seven), with a rock-ribbed face and stern habits. His first name was Ross. He never smoked. He did not drink, even coffee. One traumatic day, he came home with the news that he had lost his instructorship. Home was 2232 Haste Street, where the family had two frame houses, one behind the other, that had been partitioned into eleven apartments. For the rest of his life, Brower's father managed and janitored the apartments. Things became, in Brower's words, "pretty thin," and he remembers holes in his sweaters, holes in his shoes, and paper routes. His father's mother moved in to help with the apartments. She was a high-momentum Baptist who had seen to it that her grandson David was underwater when presented to God. She also saw to it that he always had plenty of housework to do. He washed clothes. She banned card games. She permitted the drinking of hot Jello.

The family's escape zone was the Sierra Nevada. Ross Brower had made something he called a camping box. It fitted on the running board of the Maxwell—and, later, of the Willys Knight—and it held food and utensils; one side of it let down on chains and became a table. In Berkeley, the camping box was kept in the basement, and frequently young David would go down there just to look at it. To Donner Summit was a three-day drive. (It is now a three-hour drive.) They would spend the first night in a campground in what is now metropolitan Sacramento, and the second near Colfax, on the American River. The river was potable then. As if he were there still, Brower remembers lying on the ground inside an arrangement of blankets and blanket pins—his mother at one end, his father at the other, his two brothers and his sister with him in the middle—listening to the elegiac whistling of the big Mallet engines of the Southern Pacific. He developed an extraordinary affection for trains. Malapropos as it may seem at this point in his career, he still has it. The force of nostalgia in Brower is such that it can in some instances bend logic. A railroad over the Sierra is all right. It was there. An interstate highway is an assault on the terrain.

At Donner Summit, Brower once pointed out to me the road he and his family had used. It was a dirt road seven feet wide and as tortuous as the contours of the mountains.

On almost every trip, they camped in the wild country at the south end of Lake Tahoe, in a forest of big pines, white fir. He would wade in the cold, clear, notoriously blue lake and catch minnows. He stood there one day not long ago and took in the scene as it is now. Just up the street were Jimboy's Tacos, Pettyjohn Realty, Shakey's Pizza Parlor, Harrah's casino, Harrah's Thrifty Gambler, Shell, Texaco, Phillips 66, Standard, Enco, Stoddard the Jeweler ("Wedding Rings"), and the south-shore offices of O. R. "Bode" Martin, Real Estate. We went into Harrah's Thrifty Gambler, where Brower dropped a dollar and five cents at nickel roulette and ten-cent craps, then on into the big casino. "These people were perfectly happy in Las Vegas, Carson City, and Reno," Brower said, looking around. "They didn't have to come to this lake."

I remarked that the people in Harrah's looked young and fresh-faced, and not made of ochre suède, like the people in downtown Las Vegas.

Brower said, "Maybe that's because they go out and look at the lake once in a while."

On the precise spot where Brower and his family used to camp when he was a boy now stands the Royal Valhalla Motor Lodge—Diners Club, BankAmericard, Carte Blanche, Master Charge, American Express, sunbathing balconies, and an eight-foot Anchor fence to keep undesirables away from the lake. People with oil-glistening skins were languid on the balconies.

"These are people who got on the wrong subway and missed Coney Island," Brower said. "This is Jones Beach

West. I'm glad there's a Jones Beach. I'm sorry this happened to Lake Tahoe."

Brower was standing by the Anchor fence, which had barbed wire along its top, and through it a stiff north wind was whistling. Visible through the fence were high whitecaps on the lake. The water was noticeably green. By a process called eutrophication, algae build up as a result of the accumulation of various human wastes, and even lakes that are famous for being blue will turn green. Brower said, "When Lake Erie started to die, it went in twelve years. This lake is a lot smaller than that. I can't think of a scenic climax in the world more polluted, and in more ways, than this one. Oh, is this ever grim!"

I asked him, "What do you think would happen if you were to address an audience collected out of these motels?"

"They would understand. They would be with me," he said. "People love the land."

"Do you really believe that?"

"Yes," he said. He pointed to a small bush. "Look at that plant," he said. "There has been *some* attempt at landscaping here."

"It's plastic."

"O.K.," Brower said, "I take it back. This long ago ceased to be my country anyway. You can see into my country." He pointed. "Pyramid Peak is just visible, in the Desolation Wilderness."

"Have you been up Pyramid Peak?"

"Seven times. Three times in the winter, on skis. But by

31

the time I was twenty even *that* was behind me. I found bigger peaks, wilder places, higher country."

As a child, he had at times been frightened in that country. The family had always headed south after Tahoe, into the higher mountains, higher than the Rockies—the High Sierra, tallest mountain range in the contiguous United States. To minor summits—Gaylor Peak, Sentinel Dome, Vernal Fall—the family would scramble, but David was afraid to go, and he sat in the car, sometimes trembling, while the others were away. At Glacier Point, a look-off reachable by road—and three thousand two hundred and fifty-four feet up a cliff face from the floor of Yosemite Valley—the family always went out to the lip to have a look. David stayed behind, terrified even by the thought of looking over the rim. Not many years later, though, with rope and pitons, he started up that cliff from the bottom, and he was two thousand feet off the valley floor when rocks and beer cans started to fall around him, tossed down by tourists above. Afraid for his life, he shouted until his voice was gone, but the tourists did not hear him. He says that beer cans in that situation make a light and Christmassy tinkle, while rocks go by with a Doppler effect—*peeeeenyow.* By pure luck, nothing hit him, but he was discouraged and gave up the climb.

Theodore Roosevelt, when he was President of the United States, slept one night at Glacier Point, a bit of blanket over him, and when he awoke in the morning he was covered with four inches of snow. He said later that it was the greatest day of his life. Brower told me this while we ourselves were standing at Glacier Point one day. A bronze map there

32

shows what you are looking at—Mount Starr King, Grizzly Peak, Mount Clark, Mount Lyell, Mount Maclure, Half Dome, North Dome, Clouds Rest, Mount Hoffmann, Mount Watkins, Mount Broderick, Liberty Cap. Brower had been to the summits of all these mountains. Glacier Point is a scenic climax and a half—fathoms and fathoms of air down to the green valley and up the granite on the far side to Yosemite Falls and beyond to the sharp outlines of the peaks. We shared the scene with a cluster of tourists, all adults, who were making paper airplanes and sailing them to the valley. By paper airplane, that is a long flight; and for ten, fifteen, twenty minutes at a time all these people, some of whom had driven three thousand miles to be there, kept their attention fixed on the paper airplanes. A National Park Service ranger tried to persuade them to have a look at the view. He also politely noted that what they were doing was against the law. To Brower he said that there were worse troubles than that, up there. The trail out to Glacier Point is lighted at night by fixtures placed in clefts and crevices of rock. Tourists unscrew the bulbs and throw them over the cliff.

By the time Brower reached high school, he thought that he wanted to be an entomologist, but he gave up that ambition, because at Berkeley High School people who were interested in things like entomology were considered odd. Brower had had enough of that. He was still afraid to smile, because of his teeth. As manager of the lightweight football team, he had found the beginnings of a kind of social life, and he feared losing it. He was sixteen, though, when he entered the University of California. He felt out of step, too young. Quiescent sensitivities renewed. He kept "trying for approvals here and there." He lived at home, and when he was eligible for fraternity rushing he saw from within his house one day a group from a fraternity coming up the street. They stopped and looked at the place in apparent dismay—a narrow lot in a poor section, an ersatz-Victorian clapboard-and-shingle run-down embarrassing house. The boys from the fraternity moved on without coming up the walk. Brower dropped out of the university in his sopho-more year. "Because of the Depression," he said. "The Great Depression—it was a convenient excuse." He went into the mountains. Before ten years had passed, it was being said of him that if he were to be set down at night anywhere in the Sierra Nevada, with the coming of morning he would know just where he was.

Now, at Suiattle Pass, Brower was still talking about but-terflies. He said he had raised them from time to time and had often watched them emerge from the chrysalis—first a crack in the case, then a feeler, and in an hour a butterfly. He said he had felt that he wanted to help, to speed them through the long and awkward procedure; and he had once tried. The butterflies came out with extended abdomens, and their wings were balled together like miniature clenched fists. Nothing happened. They sat there until they died. "I have never gotten over that," he said. "That kind of information is all over in the country, but it's not in town."

▲

We left the trail and went off to the right, toward Plummer Mountain, in order to attempt to find our way to the center of the area of the copper lode, and to see for ourselves—if possible—evidence of its presence. Park took the lead. The problem was to try to stay on a contour and still move in a generally westerly direction in landscape that was full of thick vegetation, ledges, ravines, and cliffs. It quickly became apparent that Brower thought Park had no idea where he was going. Our feet hurt—at least, Park's and mine did. I had developed a bone spur under one heel earlier in the year, and Park had made a bad choice with his new Canadian boots, which were stiff and were beginning to wear away parts of his ankles and feet. This fact emerged later. He said nothing at the time. Picking the shortest or easiest route—and assessing the one against the other—was of obvious importance to all of us. Although Brower seemed to be getting stronger with every added mile, he nonetheless was hardly indefatigable. Park had simply assumed command—aggressive, perhaps, because he was so uncomfortable—and we followed him, but Brower kept craning toward other possibilities, other routes. So close up, and so rough in character, the terrain was hard to read. Two or three times, Brower suggested that we try a gulch or a ridge that Park was having no part of, but Park kept moving and paid no attention, perhaps because he does not hear well. What we all feared was that we would come out onto some impossible ledge or up against a cliff face and have to turn back and add perhaps miles to our day. After a

35

time, we got into the beginnings of what appeared to be a descending, curving cul-de-sac; at least, it appeared that way to me and to Brower. We imagined that if we were to go down into it, we would end up facing cliffs and have to climb back out the way we went in. Brower said he wanted to stay on high ground and go to even higher ground to get around the problem. Park kept on walking, downhill and to his right, around the curve, whacking boulders with his pick. With no trail to keep us threaded together, we had to follow. Around the bend, the "cul-de-sac" came open, and the landscape spread out into broad alpine meadows interspersed with stands of spruce and reaching out in gentle gradients toward the talus slopes of Plummer Mountain.

This place had been named the Golf Course, apparently by explorers for Kennecott—or so we gathered from a crude property map we had with us, the "property" being the corporation's patented claims. With very little bulldozing, the Golf Course could in fact become one of the seven wonders of sport, with the red wall of Plummer Mountain above it, the deep valley of the Suiattle falling away beside it, and the sparkling, spectacular imminence of Glacier Peak in full view from every tee, fairway, and green. Brower's response to this conception was that each and every round would have to be played over his remains.

Park said that we had apparently reached the outermost lens of the copper deposit. He looked up at Plummer Mountain, all rusty and tawny and jagged in the air, and described what he was looking at as intrusive rock impregnated with pyrite and, he assumed, with copper—a porphyry of disseminated copper in granitic intrusive material. He said this mountain glacial topography reminded him of Greenland—sharp peaks sticking up through the ice pack. He could almost see the ice that had been there in the past.

Brower said he could see the hole in the ground that would be there in the future. He said that it would be a man-made crater so large it would be visible from the moon.

"Aw, Dave, it wouldn't be that bad," Park said.

While Brower was executive director of the Sierra Club, the organization became famous for bold full-page newspaper ads designed to arouse the populace and written in a style that might be called Early Paul Revere. One such ad called attention to the Kennecott Copper Corporation's ambitions in the Glacier Peak Wilderness under the headline "AN OPEN PIT, BIG ENOUGH TO BE SEEN FROM THE MOON." The fact that this was not true did not slow up Brower or the Sierra Club. In the war strategy of the conservation movement, exaggeration is a standard weapon and is used consciously on broad fronts. Beneath the headline was an aerial photograph of an open pit that Kennecott has created in Bingham Canyon, Utah. It would be difficult to exaggerate that one. Bingham Canyon is the largest copper mine in the United States. Two miles from rim to rim, it goes down into the earth in some fifty concentric circular terraces, so that from the air it looks very much like a thumbprint pressed into the ground—the thumbprint, it works out, of a man well over a hundred miles tall. The Internal Revenue Service eventually reacted to the Sierra Club ads by declaring contributions to the Sierra Club no longer tax deductible. Organizations that tried to influence legislation could not have tax-deductible status. That didn't slow up Brower, either. He went right on with the ads.

"Well, with a small telescope," Brower said.

We moved up the fairways toward Plummer Mountain, walking through buttercups and vetch. Park said cheerfully, "I wouldn't object at all to seeing a nice open pit here, improving the standard of living."

"Improving the standard of living for a short time," Brower said.

"For a hundred years," said Park. "And fifty years after that it's all covered over. There's a beach in New South Wales where the deep sands have rutile, zircon, and other rare things. National Lead and some Australian companies got permission to mine the beach. There was a hullabaloo. They mined it, and now the beach is *better* than it was before. It's been rebuilt. Swamps and mosquitoes are gone. The shorebird habitats were untouched. The Australian government wants more beaches to be mined elsewhere."

Brower let the beach go. He once wrote and narrated a film about the North Cascades, and, with "America the Beautiful" softly rendered behind his own soft-toned voice on the sound track, he said that these mountains were among "the few surviving samples of a natural world, to walk and rest in, to see, to listen to, to feel the mood of, to comprehend." The narration continued, "There isn't much of it left. What there is is all all men will ever have, and all their children. It is only as safe as people want it to be." That must have been more or less what he was thinking at that moment. At length, he said, "The pit is only a small part of what else they do."

"Every mine in the country has someone objecting to it," Park said. "Where are you going to get your metals?"

"Nevada, Arizona—Bingham Canyon."

"People object *there*."

We stepped around several piles of fresh dung. Brower said he didn't know what it was. Park said, "It's bear dung."

A pluming waterfall, hundreds of feet high, fell from the east face of Plummer Mountain, and, for lack of a more specific goal, we were homing on it.

"This scenic climax is of international significance," Brower said.

"That may be, but as long as you've got copper here, pressure to mine is going to continue."

"Well, I'll give up when copper has to be used as a substitute for gold. The kids will decide then. And I think they'll decide not to mine it."

"A mine would remove the mining area from wilderness —anyone in his right mind would admit that," Park said. "You're going to have people, equipment, machinery. You're going to blast. You're going to have a waste dump. You're also going to get copper, which contributes to the national wealth and, I think, well-being. And all that can't possibly affect Glacier Peak."

"The mine will affect anybody in this whole area who *looks* at Glacier Peak. One of the last great wildernesses in the United States would have been punctured, like a worm penetrating an apple. There would not only be the pit but also the dumps, the settling ponds, the tailings, the mill, machine shops, powerhouses, hundred-ton trucks. Good Lord! The mood would go. Wilderness defenders have to get into abstract terms like mood and so forth, but that is what it is all about. How are the people and equipment going to get in and out of here? A road? A railroad?"

"I think cost would have to enter into that."

"O.K. I put a price of ten billion dollars on the Glacier Peak Wilderness. Actually, that is facetious. There is no price. The price of beauty has never been evaluated. Look at that mountain! What would it *cost* to build an equal one?"

A galvanized pipe rising about a foot out of the earth stopped the conversation, and stopped us where we stood. Only three inches from rim to rim, it seemed somehow, to me, in the surprise of coming upon it, to reach far out into the surrounding wilderness, to be the mine itself. It had been marked as Kennecott's Drill Site No. 3. Park said it probably went down about five hundred feet, and that the core samples that had been removed through it must have been three-quarters of an inch in diameter. The core samples would have shown not only whether copper was there, in that spot, but also the concentration of it in the porphyry. Earlier in this century, if copper ore was not at least two or three per cent copper it was bypassed. Now if it is seven-tenths of one per cent copper it is mined. We sat down, roughly in a circle, around the pipe. We each had a plastic bag full of a mixture of peanuts, raisins, and chocolate, and we opened the bags and ate while we looked at the pipe, although there was so little to see. Around it spread the meadow grass, the vetch, and the buttercups, undisturbed.

"What per cent of the world's known copper is under here?" Brower asked.

"I don't know," Park said. "Kennecott hasn't told me."

For a time, the only sound was from the wind and from the waterfall on the mountain. Then Brower said, "We don't know the size of the reserve."

"That's true."

"If you start with point seven per cent and work down, say, to point three five—if that level becomes commercially feasible, then there's no telling *how* big the pit will be."

"That's true."

"The theory of economic growth is doomed on a finite planet."

"It has to be."

"We have to figure out how to cool it. I think a major change in thinking is around the corner."

Park took off his cap and smoothed his hair. "I hope your optimism holds," he said. "I'm a pessimist."

"I *have* to be an optimist. It keeps me in business. Otherwise, I'd open a waffle shop."

Of all the things Brower swallows, the two he seems to like most in the world are Tanqueray gin and whipped-cream-and-strawberry-covered waffles.

"Copper affects the international balance of payments," Park said. "We are net importers of copper."

"I can't get excited about that."

"Again, what you're saying is that you're willing to lower the standard of living."

"Very much so."

41

"Then you increase ghetto problems in cities."

"There is a gap between a lowered standard and the ghetto," Brower said. "One thing we could do, to begin with, is stop copper roofing."

"That's not a great amount. It's mostly in wiring."

"A lot of copper goes into coinage. Quarters are sandwiches of nickel and copper."

"Yes. We could get rid of that."

"We could use aluminum coins."

"Aluminum coins are horrible," Park said. "They're dirty."

"Well, then, I'd rather have a hole in a coin than a hole in Plummer Mountain. A mine in this wilderness is horrible, too."

"The mine has to come. Population pressure is irresistible."

"Population is pollution spelled inside out."

"I agree. At least, I agree that it is a very real problem."

"Families with more than two children should be taxed," Brower said.

"I agree with that, too. Everything is hopeless without population control."

"How many children do you have?"

"Three. How many do you have?"

"Four," Brower confessed.

They both turned to me.

"Four," I said.

The medical students looked on with interest.

"Seven billion people are going to be on the earth in the year 2000," Park said.

"It is wrong to assume so. Demographers make a projection like that and then we all assume it's inevitable and we go ahead and make it so."

Brower has a metaphysical or perhaps superstitious belief in the idea of the self-fulfilling prophecy. He also has no regard for the extrapolations of social scientists.

"India? Africa? Have you seen the figures?" Park asked him.

"I think there will be a massive pestilence."

"Perhaps so, but meanwhile population pressure is irresistible."

"Central Park and the Adirondacks have resisted it pretty well."

Adirondack State Park is the largest park, state or federal, in the United States. It was created in 1892, principally as the result of the efforts of a group of conservationists in Brooklyn, who put into the constitution of the State of New York this guarantee: "The Forest Preserve shall be forever kept as wild forest lands."

Park put on his cap. "There was a titanium mine in the Adirondacks during the Second World War," he said.

▲

Around the galvanized pipe, there was no evidence that copper ore had in fact come through it. We moved on. Our eyes began to hunt—in a sense, to forage—for green rock. The alpine meadows ended abruptly at the edge of an extremely steep escarpment above the stream that ran from

43

the waterfall off Plummer Mountain. We picked our way down the face of the escarpment. Park was wielding his pick with more intent than whimsy, and when he hit something we all looked around, as if we were expecting him at any moment to crack open the vaults of the Glacier Peak Wilderness. Halfway down the incline, he split off a hunk of gray rock about the size of a book and looked with interest at the part of it that was newly exposed to light.

"What did you find?"

"Nothing. Just a good streak of mineral. We're in the mineralized area."

"But no copper."

"None there. Copper is water soluble. It leaches out and precipitates below. This is certainly your ore horizon."

"Will we actually see copper ore?"

"Maybe. Who knows?"

We inched on down toward the stream, which had the pools, the clear water, the smooth water-magnified rocks, and the airy white rips of a perfect trout stream. A spring spilled into it from a ledge about eight feet above it. We paused there. Looking far up to the level where we had begun our descent to the stream, Park said, "We're locked in here now. I wouldn't go back up there for anything." Our intent was to cross the brook and try to work our way around the mountainside along a kind of welt that was known as Miner's Ridge—so named for prospectors who had worked small claims there in an era when open pits were ten feet deep.

Brower filled his Sierra Club cup and offered it to Park,

who thanked him, drank the water, and said, "If you stuck a nail in that spring and came back in two years, I think you'd have a copper nail."

"Is there copper in seawater?" I asked him.

"Very little," Park said.

"Harrison Brown thinks seawater is a viable source of copper," Brower said. "And he is considered a leading authority on resources for the future."

"That depends on who you talk to," Park said. "Anyway, I'm sure he doesn't think there is that much copper in seawater."

One of the medical students said, "Who is Harrison Brown?"

Park and Brower described Brown as a geochemist at the California Institute of Technology who believes that in energy lies the answer to the problem of diminishing resources. Minerals are almost everywhere for the taking if we can develop the energy and technology to extract them. In a mere cubic mile of seawater, for example, is more magnesium than has yet been mined in the history of metallurgy. According to Brown, uranium can be drawn from the granite of mountains. Thus, said Brower with irony, a kind of total mine could be made of the Sierra Nevada, starting at one end and consuming the entire mountain range until the area between the Nevada Desert and the orchards and vineyards of California consisted only of a vast gray peneplain.

I said that a conservationist in Seattle had told me that one method Kennecott might use to extract the copper from where we stood was to insert a nuclear bomb in Plummer

Mountain, bring the mountain down in shards into the Suiattle Valley, then pour rivers of chemicals over it to leach out the copper.

"Operation Plowshare," Park said. "It wouldn't level the mountain. That's a gross exaggeration. It would hardly show on the surface. But it wouldn't work well, either. They can't direct their blast. They make a cylinder. Most ore deposits are not cylindrical, to say the least. They're on an angle. The nuclear blast goes straight up."

Brower said, "If Harrison Brown can get so much out of granite, he ought to be able to get something out of concrete. He could start with the Embarcadero Freeway."

I once drove across the Mojave Desert with Brower; and to help pass the time in the hundred-degree heat I asked him if he could make a list of places for Harrison Brown to grind up. Where, if anywhere, would Brower find such mega-mining acceptable? "The Mojave Desert," Brower said, and then fell silent in thought. Brower's son Ken, who was twenty-three, sat up in the back seat and said, "He's hard-pressed. It's going to be a short list. He likes everything." The list was less than short. Brower began to look around the Mojave, his eyes taking in the plumbing-fixture weird-ness of the Joshua trees, the zigzag fissures in the earth, the curls and crests of desiccated waves. "I take that back," he said. "There are some nice shapes here."

In the streambed we found another galvanized pipe. This one had been bored into the earth at a forty-five-degree angle. Again there was no tangible evidence of copper. Other than the pipe, the only evidence that men had been

46

there was a number of crushed fuel cans among the boulders in the stream. A helicopter must have delivered the drill, later flying away heavy with core samples, cuprous and green. I noticed that Park was limping, and, as it happened, I was limping, too. We had a long way to go even to return to the trail, let alone to reach the place where we had planned to stop for the night, a scenic climax of much renown—Image Lake, a mirror-surfaced mountain tarn so situated that it reflects and even magnifies Glacier Peak. Park was not much interested in going there, since a detour would be involved. Brower felt that the lake should not be missed. Meanwhile, we would hunt for copper along Miner's Ridge, which at that point was the most uninviting piece of terrain I had ever seen, being thickly vegetated, trailless, chopped with rock walls and ravines, and generally so steep that the use of hands would obviously be necessary most of the way. Park moved quite slowly, hunting the best route, making his way downhill, breaking through meshed branches, and continually chipping at rocks. Somehow, he and I became separated from the others. We shouted and heard them shout back. They were above and behind us. We waited for them to join us.

Park said, "Dave lives in a house, doesn't he?" Park had a grin in the corner of his mouth, and I developed one in mine. I told him I had once heard a man in an audience in Scarsdale tell Brower that to be consistent with his philosophy he should wear a skin and live in a cave.

I thought of Brower's house and how it clings to a steep hillside far above the campus at Berkeley. It is a simple structure, made of redwood. Although it is far from large, it almost completely fills Brower's lot, which he acquired in 1946, at the start of the postwar building boom. He sketched a plan on the back of an envelope, showed it to a contractor, and told him to build what he saw—thus the first house in what quickly became a neighborhood. There is almost no front yard—just a concrete apron for Brower's Volvo and his Volkswagen bus. In back is a patch of ground, Brower's private claim on the out-of-doors—the eighty-seventh part of an acre. Filled with vegetation—loquat, lemon, fuchsia, apricot, peach, camellia—it is an infinitesimal jungle. From the front windows of Brower's house the view of San Francisco Bay is panoptic—the Golden Gate, the Bay Bridge, the Marin Peninsula, the white city—and would be a breathtaking view were it not for a high telephone pole, directly across the street, where lines come in from four or five directions and have been looped and bunched into something that suggests a huge tumbleweed hanging in the air, an enormous ganglion of copper wires.

"Yes, he does live in a house," I said.

We could hear Brower and the medical students crashing through the undergrowth and coming closer to us.

"Is it painted?" Park asked. "Most people don't think about pigments in paint. Most white-paint pigment now is titanium. Red is hematite. Black is often magnetite. There's chrome yellow, molybdenum orange. Metallic paints are a little more permanent. The pigments come from rocks in the ground. Dave's electrical system is copper, probably from Bingham Canyon. He couldn't turn on a light or make ice without it. The nails that hold the place together come from

48

the Mesabi Range. His downspouts are covered with zinc that was probably taken out of the ground in Canada. The tungsten in his light bulbs may have been mined in Bishop, California. The chrome on his refrigerator door probably came from Rhodesia or Turkey. His television set almost certainly contains cobalt from the Congo. He uses aluminum from Jamaica, maybe Surinam; silver from Mexico or Peru; tin—it's still in tin cans—from Bolivia, Malaya, Nigeria. People seldom stop to think that all these things— planes in the air, cars on the road, Sierra Club cups—once, somewhere, were rock. Our whole economy—our way of doing things, most of what we have, even our culture—rests on these things. Oh, gad! I haven't even mentioned minerals like manganese and sulphur. You won't make steel without them. You can't make *paper* without sulphur. By a country's use of sulphuric acid you can almost measure its industrial capacity. The top of Mount Adams has been prospected by sulphur companies. Did you know that?"

Mount Adams is one of the great beauties of the Cascades, a volcano of the storybook kind, its curving lines sweeping to a white summit. The mountain is owned by the government of the United States, but its apex could be mined. The top is where the sulphur is.

Brower and the medical students caught up with us, and Brower asked how we were doing.

"Fine," said Park. "But, to tell you the truth, I wish these boots were still in Canada. My feet are in bad shape."

"Did you find any copper?" one of the medical students asked.

Park shook his head. "It's down in here, though," he said,

pointing straight down. "That's for sure." With no trail, and without much energy, we continued along the face of Miner's Ridge, and the going became even slower as we encountered a greater concentration of ravines, but no copper. The desire to see evidence of the copper lode was mere curiosity —no one doubted that copper was inside the mountain—but the curiosity, the sense of hunting, was compelling nonetheless.

Park talked about minerals. Few minerals are found in their native state, or, as he put it, free in nature; among them are silver, platinum, and gold. Zinc comes from sphalerite, tin comes from cassiterite, cobalt comes from smaltite, mercury comes from cinnabar. Each year, in the United States, about fifteen hundred tons of silver—about a third of all that is used—goes into photographic film and paper. For the price of a pound of hamburger, you can buy ten pounds of steel, and if it were not that cheap there would be economic problems all over the earth. Vanadium comes from sedimentary rock and may be an answer to air pollution; vanadium somehow defeats the toxicity in exhaust fumes. Titanium exists in the rutile of Georgia and Florida beaches, and is needed for the skins of supersonic aircraft, because aluminum without titanium would melt in the friction heat. Almost all mercury comes from three places: Almadén, Idria, Monte Amiata (Spain, Yugoslavia, Italy). Mercury is essential to any instrument intended to measure or control temperature or pressure. There is no known substitute for it, and there is very little of it. Japan buys iron ore from Nevada and coal from strip mines in West Virginia. In many places in the United States, it is impossible to buy nails that

50

were not made in Japan. No nation has an adequate supply of all the minerals it uses. Since 1900, more minerals have been used than in all previous time.

Park had recently published all this, in less random form, in a book titled *Affluence in Jeopardy*, which is in part a primer on minerals and their uses and significance and in part an exhortation to mankind to husband what we have. Introducing minerals one by one, he says in clear and fascinating detail what they are, where they come from, what we do with them, and, ultimately, how we are locked into a system of living that is fuelled by them and founded upon them and would collapse without them. He quotes Lord Dewar, who said, "Minds are like parachutes. They only function when they are open," and he goes on to define conservation (at least with regard to minerals) as the complete use of natural resources, with as little waste as possible, for the benefit of all the people, and not merely for industrialists, on the one hand, or preservationists, on the other. He says that the search for energy, being vital to the extraction of minerals, and thus to the survival of the society, is far more important than exploration of the back of the moon, and he says that each nation should have a mineral policy that involves the intelligent exploration and development of mineral resources and an acceptance of fully reciprocal international trade. Copper, he reports, is used in the United States at the rate of at least two million tons a year. "As we look at the nonferrous metals, we note that, in spite of the value of mercury and the great demands for aluminum, copper remains the giant of the group. There has been an unbelievable amount of searching for copper, much of it in recent years, and there are entire nations whose economies depend upon this metal. . . . No substitute for copper is as satisfactory as the metal itself."

At about half past three that afternoon, we came to a small stream that ran straight down the steep mountainside. We shook off our packs, removed our boots, and set our feet in the water. "Oh, gad, that feels good," Park said. Our feet were as white as fish flesh in the cold water—so cold that I could barely stand it. This was a way to keep going, though. A cold stream offers a kind of retread. The pain goes away for a while afterward, and miles can be added to a day. Reaching upstream, Brower dipped himself a cupful of water. "Wilderness is worth it, if for no other reason than it is the last place on earth where you can get good water," he said. No one else said anything. We were too tired. We stared into the stream, or looked across the deep Suiattle Valley at the virgin forests on the lower slopes and the snow and ice on the upper slopes of Glacier Peak. Park's attention became fixed on the pebbles at the bottom of the stream, and after a moment he leaned forward and reached into the water, wetting his sleeve. He removed from the water a blue-and-green stone about the size of a garden pea. He set it on the palm of one hand and passed it before us. "We have been looking all day for copper," he said. "Here it is."

▲

The beauty of the mountain across the valley was cool and absolute, but the beauty of the stone in Park's hand was

52

warm and subjective. It affected us all. Human appetites, desires, ambitions, greeds, and profound aesthetic and acquisitional instincts were concentrated between the stone and our eyes. Park reached again into the stream, and said, "Here's another one. The blue is chrysocolla—copper silicate. The rest is malachite—green copper carbonate."

All of us, Brower included, knelt in the stream and searched for stones. Brower found one. He was obviously excited by it. Brigham found one. Snow found one. Park found one as large as a robin's egg, mottled blue and green, with black specks of cupric oxide.

"My God, look at that!"

"Malachite and chrysocolla in altered intrusive rock," Park said.

"I've got another one," Brower said. "Good Lord, look at them all!"

"Hey, there are even more up here!" Snow called out.

"The rock is probably monzonite—a granite with equal parts of potash and soda feldspars—altered by hydrothermal solutions. I'd have to take it into a lab to know for sure. The copper came way up out of the earth's core when these mountains were fluid."

Larry Snow was shouting from above. He had a green rock in his hand the size of a golf ball. The slope and the streambed were as steep as a ladder, and ten minutes earlier the thought of going up there would have filled me with gloom and inertia. Now I put on my boots and followed him, scrambling hand over foot for the copper.

The higher we went, the larger were the green rocks—

two inches, three inches, four inches thick. On a ledge about a hundred yards above Park, Brower, and Brigham, who were still assembling green pebbles, Snow picked up a rock that he could barely manage with one hand. Others like it were all over the ledge—cuprous green and aquamarine.

I held one high in my right hand and shouted down to Brower, "Dave, look at this! Look at this rock! Don't you think it would be a crime against society not to take this copper out of here?"

"Stay up there! Don't come back down!" Brower shouted. He was a small figure, from that high perspective. He was waving Snow and me away. "Stay up there! We'll send a party for you next spring!"

At the back of the ledge was the source of the copper. A deep, narrow hole had been blown into the side of the mountain, making what appeared to be a small cave—a nick in the wilderness, exposing and fragmentarily spilling its treasure. Snow and I filled a small canvas bag with perhaps twenty pounds of ore and made our way back down the streambed.

No one seemed anxious to move. I again took off my boots and put my feet in the stream. Brower had made an attractive collection of green pebbles. He looked with interest and feigned contempt at the big stones we had brought down. Brower is a collector of rocks. Behind his desk in his office in San Francisco were rocks he had collected from all over, and notably from the canyons of the Colorado—Glen Canyon, Grand Canyon. In most cases, he did not know what these rocks were, nor did he appear to care. He had taken them for their beauty alone.

Park was contemplating Glacier Peak. We were as close to it as we would ever be. It was right there—so enormous that it seemed to be on top of us, extending upward five thousand feet above our heads. "That's the sort of thing that draws people into geology," he said. "Geologists go into the field because of love of the earth and of the out-of-doors."

"The irony is that they go into wilderness and change it," Brower said.

Park appeared to be too tired to be argumentative. "There are some silly things about the mining laws," he said after a time, and he went on to explain that once a mining company or anyone else establishes a patented claim on public land they have complete rights to do anything they want, just as if they—and not the people of the United States—were owners of the property. Within federal law, they can cut down all the trees, they can build skyscrapers. If Kennecott wants to, Kennecott can put up a resort hotel in the Glacier Peak Wilderness. This law, enacted in 1872, makes no sense now to Park. He said he thought that mining companies should be given leases, and that these leases should include strong restrictions on mining practice and use of the land. In his view, something like that would go a long way toward eliminating the dichotomy that currently exists between conservationists and miners. While he was saying all this, he dried his feet in the air. I noticed for the first time that Park's heels were so raw red they were all but bleeding. He pulled on his socks and, with care, his boots.

He got up—we all got up—and moved west along the ridge. He was forced to trudge, even after we rejoined the trail. Going to Image Lake would add several miles to the trip, involve an extra climb, and, the next day, a precipitous descent, but when the trail forked, Park headed for Image Lake.

Above Park's desk at Stanford was a picture of a jackass, with the caption "Can I help? Or do you want to make your own mistakes?" Near it was a photostatic blowup of a five-cent postage stamp showing cherry boughs and the Jefferson Memorial over the legend "Plant a More Beautiful America." Park's great-grandfather was a Minuteman. His grandfather was a guide on the Santa Fe Trail. His father had a real-estate and travel agency in Wilmington. His older brother went off and became a cowpuncher for the Bell Ranch, in New Mexico, and this in part established the draw to the West that Park felt throughout his youth. Tall, loose, rangy, and graceful, Park was a basketball player—a very good one—and he loved the game so much that he played not only for Wilmington High School (he was in the Class of 1922) but also, on the side, for various churches. His father told him that he had to worship at any church for which he played basketball, so for a long time he went to church at least twice each Sunday. He says he hasn't been to church since, except on the day that he was married. Also in those days, he made camping trips along the Brandywine, fished with a drop line in Chesapeake Bay, collected rocks that people sent him from beyond the hundredth meridian, and waited for the day when he could go beyond it himself.

When he was eighteen, he went to New York and shipped out in steerage on a Matson Line steamer for Galveston. It was the cheapest way West. He was not sure where he was going. He thought he might go to Golden (the Colorado School of Mines), or possibly to Socorro (the New Mexico School of Mines). "In those days, if you wanted to go to one of those places all you had to do was show up," he once explained to me. Eventually, he showed up at Socorro. He was the captain of his college basketball team, and he learned his mineralogy, and went on to get his master's degree at the University of Arizona and his Ph.D. at the University of Minnesota. In mining camps in those years, he became known as Chas (pronounced "chass"), specifically because the nickname distinguished him from the numerous Chinese in the mining camps, who, to a man, were known as Charlie. For a time, he worked as a mine surveyor for the New Jersey Zinc Company in Hanover, New Mexico, where he met a girl from Colorado—Eula Blair—who eventually became his wife and the mother of his two sons and his daughter. His daughter is a teacher of physical education. His sons are both working geologists—one with Humble Oil, the other with Hanna Mining. Mining geology is not widely taught anymore, and across the years students have come from all over the earth to Stanford because—in term, anyway, when he was not in equatorial Africa or the Andes or the Great Basin or the Black Hills—Park has been there, to teach them courses with names like Ore Genesis 101.

We were about a mile east of Image Lake. Park stopped, picked up a stone, split it in half with his pick, and said, "We are well past the mineral deposit. The mine won't come anywhere near Image Lake. The rock here is not intrusive. It's completely volcanic."

"Of course, it could be a volcanic overburden," said Brower, to suggest the possibility that far beneath the earth's surface the copper might spread to untold dark horizons.

"That's true. It could," Park said, with a tired shrug, and he trudged on.

▲

We were a somewhat bizarre group on arrival at Image Lake. Park and I could scarcely place one foot after the other. The medical students appeared to be as fresh as they had been in the morning. And Brower was yodelling with pleasure. Brower yodels badly. The happier he seems to be, the more and the worse he yodels. He is Antaeus in the mountains, and he was clearly feeling good.

Image Lake is very small—a stock-water pond in size—and it stands in open and almost treeless terrain. Slowly, we went around it, looking for a place to sleep. The sun was just setting, and we had arrived much too late. We walked past tents along the shore—blue tents, green tents, red tents, orange tents. The evening air was so still that we could hear voices all around the lake. We heard transistor radios. People greeted us as we went by. The heaviest shadows were in the northwest arc of the shore, so the air was particularly cold there, and space had been left. We took the space. We had come into the mountains from the east. These people had come in from the west. It had not been an easy trip for them, to be sure. The nearest roadhead was fifteen miles west of us and some four thousand feet below. Nonetheless, the lake that night had the ambience of a cold and crowded oasis. Shivering, I climbed up a slope to witness in the water the fading image of the great mountain. Objectively, the reflection was all it was said to be. But a "No Vacancy" sign seemed to hang in the air over the lake.

A real sign pointed the way to a privy. We collected firewood, which was very hard to find, and when we had something of a blaze going and had all drawn in close around it for warmth, I said to Park and Brower, "Do you feel that you're in a wilderness now?"

"Yes," Brower said. "All these people certainly diminish the wilderness experience, but I've seen crowds in wilderness before. I know that they'll go away, and when they go they haven't really left anything."

Once, on a trail in the Sierra, Brower and I passed numerous hikers coming in the other direction, and because there were so many of them they disturbed him. They weren't riding Bonanza Trail-Bikes and they didn't have transistor radios and they weren't tossing beer cans away. They were disturbing to him only because they were there. Brower kept asking them if we were likely to find "too many" people in Humphreys Basin, which lay ahead of us, and when he concluded that Humphreys Basin—an area of several thousand acres—was going to contain too much of humankind he left the trail and struck off overland for another part of the mountains. Once, also, Brower and I were approaching the Sierra from the west on Route 198, and it happened to be the evening of the final day of a holiday weekend, and a river of cars was coming in the other direction. Brower drove without hurry. "The longer we wait, the more people we'll get out of the mountains," he said.

Now, at Image Lake, Park said, "This is no wilderness to me. My idea of wilderness is not to walk a quarter of a mile to a biffy. There's just too many people here."

Brower said, "It's hard to believe that this many people would walk this far."

"Population pressure," Park said. "You can't stop it. I don't really understand why they come here, though. This is a very ordinary little mountain lake."

We put our dinner into a single pot, boiled the food, ate it; and no one noticed what it was. Park was the first to speak again. "The more I see of this country, the more I fail to see what that copper mine would do to it. When we started, I was under the impression it might do something, but, golly, I can't see that now."

"The excavation would be within a mile of here and would effectively remove even this lake from wilderness. Right now it has more impact than it can bear. The ecosystem is delicate here. Recovery rates are fast, but nonetheless it is getting pounded. And the disruption would go all the way to Suiattle Pass, so the Glacier Peak Wilderness would effectively be cut in half."

"There would be a mining company here on business, and that's what they'd be doing—that's all. The miners would stick to the mine. Some would go off hiking or fishing, sure, but they would be doing that anyway. Miners like wilderness."

"The trouble is they want to dig it up and take it home."

"Awww."

"Logging follows mining."

"You can control that."

"That's what I'm hoping."

"Your idea of control is to keep it out."

"All a conservation group can do is to defer something. There's no such thing as a permanent victory. After we win a battle, the wilderness is still there, and still vulnerable. When a conservation group *loses* a battle, the wilderness is dead."

"It doesn't have to be."

"It's dead by definition."

"I don't agree with that concept of wilderness—to just take a big block of land and say you're going to keep it for the future. I can't see it."

"Wilderness was originally a nice place to go to, but that is not what wilderness is for. Wilderness is the bank for the genetic variability of the earth. We're wiping out that reserve at a frightening rate. We should draw a line right now. Whatever is wild, leave it wild."

"I would take a certain area and make part of it accessible and part of it inaccessible. Taking very large areas out of the country and keeping them as they were a thousand years ago—you can't do it. The population pressure is too great."

"A wilderness is a place where natural forces can keep

working essentially uninterrupted by man. If ten per cent is still wild, we should tithe with it. Man has taken enough for himself already. We should pretend the rest doesn't exist. It's there for a different purpose."

"What purpose?"

"Not man's purpose. Man is a recent thing in the time scale here."

The moon had risen, pale and gibbous. We looked up at it. Men had been there recently and were going back in a few weeks. "There may be possibilities in the moon, but I can't see it," Park said.

"Apollo 11 proved the capability, and that was quite enough," Brower said. "Now let's spend the money on something else. We need to save the earth."

"Moon walking is silly," Park agreed. "There are too many things about the earth that we don't know, that would improve our lot, and that cost a lot of money."

"We're not so poor that we have to spend our wilderness or so rich that we can afford to. That kind of boxes it in nicely. Newton Drury said it."

"I don't believe you can stop expansion of the consumption of raw materials."

"You stop when you run out," said Brower. "Meanwhile, you make it less wasteful."

"Waste is criminal."

"If we recycled enough copper annually, we could do without this mine. Now that we know that we ourselves are on a spaceship, we have to get into our heads a concept of limits. Some things must stop or the world will become repugnant. There are limits everywhere, whether we are dealing with an island, a river, a mountain, with people, or with air. Living diversity is the thing we're preserving."

The fire had subsided almost to nothing, and the conversation subsided with it. The air was quite cold. We dispersed and got into our sleeping bags. Brower had arranged his pallet on top of a high promontory above the lake-shore. As a mountaineer, he knew that less dew condenses on high ground, and also that the air is warmer there. Park and I felt too achingly sore in the feet to bother making the climb. We stretched out below. As Park adjusted himself to the ground beneath him, he said, "I know half a dozen lakes like this that I can drive to and where I would find less people. I'll give you my interest in Image Lake for a piece of a counterfeit penny." Then he fell asleep. It was 8:30 P.M.

▲

Once, in the Black Hills, Park had taken me with him into the deepest mine in the Western Hemisphere. The descent took one hour—first in a wire cage down a shaft almost a mile deep, then a level mile or so on a narrow-gauge railway, then on down in another cage, until we were six thousand eight hundred feet beneath the earth's surface. Heat increases in that area about two degrees for every three hundred feet you go down into the earth. The rock down there was a hundred and twenty degrees Fahrenheit, but the temperature in the tunnels we walked through had been brought down into the nineties by air pumped from the surface in long cloth tubes. The tunnels are known as drifts. Wearing coveralls, rubber boots, lamps, hard hats, and shatterproof glasses, we followed one drift to its end—to the deepest and remotest working face in the mine. Park hit away with his pick. Sparks came off the wall, and so did pieces of rock, basically dark gray with shining seams of pyrite and nodular insets of white quartz. I still have the pieces of rock that he knocked off that wall, and I have often shown them to people—particularly to children—and asked them what they thought they were looking at. What is in that rock? Why would men dig a hole that deep? What would make them go six thousand eight hundred feet underground? What could they possibly be seeking? The answer seldom comes quickly, perhaps because the rock is truly prosaic. "Iron?" they say. "Copper?" "Silver?" No. Keep going. It is the sum and symbol of why we mine anything, the base substance of the economies of nations, the malleable, ductile, most saint-seducing mineral in the crust of the earth. Something happens in their eyes when at last they say, "Gold."

Another day, on the surface, Park went out to look for greenstone pillows in a hill of amphibolite. Someone in the Geological Survey had suggested that these rock pillows, by the way they were positioned in the folds of the Black Hills, could indicate the direction of gold. Park walked along a ledge on the face of an escarpment, nagging at the pillows with his pick. Finally, he said, "Pretty inconclusive, I'd say." We were on high ground, and we could see around that beautiful country, with its big pines and its Engelmann's spruce so dark, dark green that the Sioux called the hills black. Surrounded by hot, dry terrain—the South Dakota Badlands on one side of them and Wyoming on the other— the Black Hills reach seven thousand feet and are cool and moist, with green valleys and clear-stream waterfalls and beaver ponds and deer and trout. "The Sioux loved this country," Park said. "No wonder they didn't want to give it up."

Land was a form of religion to the Indians, and the Black Hills, in this sense, were the religion of the Sioux. With all the fish, game, and beauty any man could want, the Black Hills fed the Sioux in body and spirit. Indians had no sense of private property, private land. The idea of individual human beings' owning pieces of the earth was to them at first incomprehensible and, when comprehended, a form of sacrilege. With the white man and his sense of property and the rights of property came the inequities and paradoxes that eventually led to the need for a conservation move-ment. Meanwhile, in 1851 the Sioux were promised by treaty that they could keep their Black Hills forever. In 1874, white men found gold there, and in 1875 white men entered the Black Hills in staggering numbers—white trash, in the main, like Wild Bill Hickok. It was the last gold rush in the United States. The promise to the Sioux was perma-nently broken, and the Sioux expressed their grief by de-stroying General Custer and his soldiers. "The Sioux are now a hundred miles east of here on a flat reservation in the Badlands," Park said to me. "There are no Sioux in the Sierra Club."

As we walked through a narrow swale filled with lilies, daisies, horsemint, and yellow vetch, we passed depressions in the ground that appeared to be graves that had been dug but not filled. Kinnikinnick berries grew in these depressions, and in one grew an aspen, tall and spreading, and in all likelihood nearly a hundred years old. "Prospectors," Park said. "A man would have come here and spent a day or a day and a half digging that hole in the ground. If he found anything, that would be his discovery-point pit, around which he would stake his claim. It was hit or miss. He had little to go on but the association of gold with quartz and pyrite. Sometimes prospectors found nuggets the size of peanuts. But that was extremely rare. Mining, and panning in the streams, was generally very hard work." There was a cool wind in the ponderosas, and a long view down through the stands of aspen below them. The rock formation before us stood on end. "It's Pre-Cambrian," Park said. "It's between three and four billion years old, probably. There are some old Pre-Cambrian flows like this up in Michigan—old pillow flows. There's some Pre-Cambrian rock in the Berkshires. There's also some in the bottom of the Grand Canyon. Look there! There are two good pillows! Maybe that boy has something."

The Black Hills are veined with unpaved roads. One of them was the stage route, a hundred years ago, from Telegraph Gulch to Deadwood. Driving his car along it one afternoon, Park said, "This is what I like about my profession. You see so much beautiful country. If I were starting over again, I'd do the same thing." In the next few miles, he saw

66

a night hawk, a white-winged junco, a vesper sparrow, a western flycatcher, and a Townsend solitaire. He is a member of the American Ornithologists Union. He is a man who knows what he is looking at in wild country. I have never spent time with anyone who was more aware of the natural world, and he seemed to find in the land and landscape of the Black Hills an expression of almost everything he had come to believe about that world. He said, "People have a tendency to get a little bit emotional about preservation of the environment, I'm afraid. There are a couple of sawmills in here. They take mature trees. What harm do they do? They don't hurt the country. I don't see it. While I love the out-of-doors, I have no use for wilderness. We need to lumber. We need to mine. People don't realize what mining is. They don't realize the contributions that minerals and metals make to their lives. You can't live without industry. But that is what preservationists will say. Sawmills, mines, and forests *can* live together. These forests are beautiful here. They really are. The Black Hills are an example of where industry has not ruined an environment." In Park's view, about all that has been ruined in the Black Hills is Mount Rushmore, where the face of a mountain was blasted away and replaced with the faces of four American Presidents. It happens that Jefferson's nose is cracking. So is Lincoln's chin. And there are water stains on George Washington. But all that is just added insult. No face should be there except the face of the mountain. Even now, the face of Chief Crazy Horse is being sculpted on a mountain nearby. The Sioux need no monuments. Their monuments are seven thousand feet high and have been there since Pre-Cambrian time.

The deep gold mine is all that lives on from the legends of Deadwood Gulch. Park, a director of the mining company, was in the Black Hills to make a model—a sort of cubic map—of the mine. Three metamorphic-rock formations, called Homestake, Ellison, and Poorman, are folded together there like three kinds of ice cream. The gold is in the Homestake. From established drifts, narrow drills "feel" their way into the rock, sometimes as far as fifteen hundred feet—strange antennae. With data so obtained, Park was reproducing on stacked plastic sheets all the streaks, striations, bands, and brindles in several cubic miles of rock.

Down on the Sixty-eight—as the sixty-eight-hundred-foot level of the mine is called—Park looked with admiration at the walls of a drift and said, "These miners can look at a turn in a drift and tell who made it. They're proud of a good drift, clean walls. These are hard-rock miners, not coal miners. And they want you to know the difference. There are advantages in mining. Conditions are fixed. Man has control of the environment. People who work in a mine figure they are creating something. They feel that they are creating wealth. They all think they're geologists. There isn't a miner here who doesn't have a favorite place he wants to blast into."

Park drew a couple of miners into the conversation, which was spoken in high voices, because of the noise of the air pumps and the working drills. "I prefer working underground to on the surface," one of them said. "Conditions are

68

set. You're not going to get caught in a thunderstorm. If I didn't like it, I wouldn't be doing it. We're tearing apart solid rock."

The rock, Park explained, is taken to the surface and crushed until it is fine sand. Mercury is poured through the sand. The mercury adroitly picks up gold, and nothing else. The mercury is then boiled away. Cyanide is poured into the sand and dissolves from it even more gold. Zinc is then put into the gold-cyanide solution. The zinc dissolves, and replaces the gold, which falls as metal to the bottom. The sand is put back in the mine, where concrete is poured on it to make platforms for upward mining. Thus, the mine consumes its own tailings, sparing in large measure the beauty of its environment—but not sparing it entirely. Because crushed rock expands in volume, all cannot be put back into the mine, and one of the Black Hills is a flat-topped mountain of black sand. And, as it happens, Whitewood Creek flows black after it passes the mine.

Park said that three tons of rock yield only one ounce of gold—a bit of gold about the size of a drop of rain. There is only about a third of an ounce of gold to back the financial wherewithal of each person now on earth. The very name Fort Knox implies vast vaults and armories full of piled gold, but actually the gold in Fort Knox could be formed into a twenty-foot cube. All the gold in all the monetary reserves of the world could be stacked on a single tennis court and scarcely reach over the fence.

Now, on the ground by Image Lake in the North Cascades, Park had begun to snore. To block the dew, we had stretched a clear-plastic tarpaulin over our heads, and I lay on my back and looked up through it at the disrupted constellations. I remembered walking into Park's living room once in Palo Alto. What I had noticed first, on a coffee table, was a book called *Gold, Its Beauty, Power, and Allure.*

▲

In the morning, we went down to the Suiattle River—a drop of three thousand feet from Image Lake down the face of Miner's Ridge on a grassy incline so steep that Brower began telling stories about what happens to people on slopes like that if they fall. They apparently start to tumble, and sometimes can't stop. Park said he didn't care whether he fell or not—he was that uncomfortable. He finally took off his boots and put on his open leather sandals, deciding that bruises all over his feet would be preferable to the pain in his heels. His difficulty notwithstanding, he kept knocking rocks apart all day. After the big drop, the trail, for something like ten miles, ran roughly parallel to the river. The more altitude we gave up, the larger were the trees, the deeper the forest, until we were walking among big Douglas firs six feet thick. The air was warm and sunlit, and even when we could not see the river through the dense trees, the Suiattle was something to hear. It had the overbearing sound of rock sliding in a steel chute. As the afternoon lengthened, the sound grew louder. Park said he had known rivers in Alaska that could be crossed in the morning but by

70

afternoon were unfordable torrents of melted glacier ice. "This one is like them," he said. Coming into view, the Suiattle was a headlong chaos of standing waves and swirling eddies, white with spray and glacial flour. "This one is a really wild river," Park went on. "Look at that rush of glacier milk."

The lower reaches of the trail had been scarred and battered by an improvement project commissioned by the United States Forest Service. Dynamite had torn great rocks apart, and some of the big trees had been felled to make the trail wider and the grade easier. Brower began to say unflattering things about the Forest Service, which he described as a collection of timber engineers who have no concept of ecology and whose idea of selective logging is to select a mountain and cut all the trees down. He said, "We conservationists would like to keep the Forest Service out of wilderness, and, for that matter, the National Park Service, too. They build too many things for their own convenience —for rangers who have forgotten how to range."

Brower had scarcely said this when we came upon a man who had three horses with him and several empty dynamite boxes. He was about thirty-five, strongly built and in excellent condition, solid muscles under his T-shirt, short-cropped hair, pale-gray eyes. His name was Don Dayment, and he told us he had been the foreman of the crew that improved the trail. Brower complained bluntly about the desecration of the trail. Dayment looked from Brower to Park to me to the medical students, and he said, "You wilderness-lovers are all the same."

"You foresters are all the same," Brower said.

Dayment cinched his horses. "Wherever man goes, whatever he does, he scars the land," he said. "That's the way things are. We were told to make a ten-per-cent grade here with a two-foot tread and eight feet of clearance. If we had to chop a six-foot fir, too bad."

I asked him where he lived, and he said he had been born twenty miles from where we stood.

I asked him how he felt about the copper mine.

"I don't like it, and I'll tell you why," he said. "I don't like the class of people that would come with it. I've seen their camps—in Wallace, Idaho, and Butte, Montana. They're dirty and run-down, and so are the people. I wouldn't want my children growing up around them."

Over the last five miles, each of us went at his own pace; we gave up all cohesion as a group. I walked with Brower, who was moving fast, because I had the almost drunken, rubber-legged feeling you get toward the finish of a long, long walk, and the roadhead at the end of the trail had become for me a repeating mirage. The trail ran closer and closer to the Suiattle—right beside it in some stretches—and the sound of the water was deafening. Over what proved to be the last thousand yards, though, we became aware of a sound even louder than the sound of the river—a higher-pitched roar, coming in jugular gusts, and increasing in volume as we moved down the trail. We came to the roadhead. There in the river, in the middle of the river, the white torrents crashing over it, was a bulldozer. Half submerged, its purpose obscure, it heaved, belched, backed, shoved, and lurched around on the bottom of the Suiattle as if the water were not there. The bulldozer was stronger than the river.

I took off my boots and sat alone on a ledge where my feet could reach the water. For a couple of hours, I had been able to think of almost nothing but feet. Now the cold milk of glaciers dispelled that, and as I watched the bulldozer my mind went back over the day—all the way back to its beginning. Miner's Ridge, as it extended westward from Image Lake, was a ridge indeed. The terrain fell away as steeply on the north side as it did toward the Suiattle, and we had walked for a mile or so—before beginning the descent—along the ridgeline of a topographical configuration that was like a sharply pitched gable roof. There was no timber up there, and in the early morning the ridge was isolated from the land below by huge bodies of cloud that filled up the river valleys on either side almost to our shoes. Above the clouds, the air was clear and the sky blue, and nothing else broke into that world but Glacier Peak, seven miles away—all ice and snow, and almost too dazzling to look at as it sprayed sunlight in every direction. Big blueberries were growing along the trail, and we began to eat them as if we had had no breakfast. Some were a half inch in diameter. Filling his Sierra Club cup with berries, Brower said, "I'm just taking the renewable crop. Only bears will object."

Park ate his blueberries straight from the bushes. His eyes lifted suddenly and followed a bird in flight above the ridge. He said, "Look at that marsh hawk. What's *he* doing up here?" The hawk canted to its left and soared in the direction of Glacier Peak. Streamers of cloud began to rise from the Suiattle Valley, cross the face of the mountain, and above the summit disappear, sparkling, into the blue. Park said it was a shame that more people couldn't see Glacier Peak—in fact, he thought people had a right to see it—and a nice little mining road would take care of that.

Brower said that a view of Glacier Peak, to mean much of anything, ought properly to be earned, and that the only way to earn it was to get to it on foot.

"What about people who can't walk?" Park said.

"They stay home. Ninety-nine point nine per cent can walk—if they want to."

"The other one-tenth per cent includes my wife."

Without hesitating, Brower said, "I have a friend named Garrett Hardin, who wears leg braces. I have heard him say that he would not want to be able to come to a place like this by road, and that it is enough for him just to know that these mountains exist as they are, and he hopes that they will be like this in the future."

"The future can take care of itself," Park said. "I don't condone waste, but I am not willing to penalize present people. I say they're penalized if they don't have enough copper. Dave says they're penalized if they don't have enough wilderness. Right?" He smacked a stone with his pick.

"Right," said Brower. "But I go further. I believe in wilderness for itself alone. I believe in the rights of creatures other than man. And I suppose I accept Nancy Newhall's definition: 'Conservation is humanity caring for the future.'

74

It is the antithesis of 'Eat, drink, and be merry, for tomorrow we die.'"

"These are the best blueberries I've ever seen," Park said. "Here on Miner's Ridge."

Brower's cup was up to its brim, and before he ate any himself he passed them among the rest of us. It was a curious and surpassingly generous gesture, since we were surrounded by bushes that were loaded with berries. We all accepted.

"I just feel sorry for all you people who don't know what these mountains are good for," Brower said.

"What are they good for?" I said.

"Berries," said Brower.

And Park said, "Copper."

PART 2

An Island

David Brower, who talks to groups all over the country about conservation, refers to what he says as The Sermon. He travels so light he never seems far from home—one tie, one suit. He calls it his preacher suit. He has given the sermon at universities, in clubs, in meeting halls, and once in a cathedral (he has otherwise not been in a church for thirty years), and while he talks he leans up to the lectern with his feet together and his knees slightly bent, like a skier. He seems to feel comfortable in the stance, perhaps because he was once a ski mountaineer.

Sooner or later in every talk, Brower describes the creation of the world. He invites his listeners to consider the six days of Genesis as a figure of speech for what has in fact been four billion years. On this scale, a day equals something like six hundred and sixty-six million years, and thus "all day Monday and until Tuesday noon, creation was busy getting the earth going." Life began Tuesday noon, and "the beautiful, organic wholeness of it" developed over the next four days. "At 4 P.M. Saturday, the big reptiles came on. Five hours later, when the redwoods appeared, there were no more big reptiles. At three minutes before midnight, man appeared. At one-fourth of a second before midnight, Christ arrived. At one-fortieth of a second before midnight, the Industrial Revolution began. We are surrounded with people who think that what we have been doing for that one-fortieth of a second can go on indefinitely. They are considered normal, but they are stark, raving mad."

Brower holds up a photograph of the world—blue, green, and swirling white. "This is the sudden insight from Apollo," he says. "There it is. That's all there is. We see through the eyes of the astronauts how fragile our life is, how thin is the epithelium of the atmosphere."

Brower has computed that we are driving through the earth's resources at a rate comparable to a man's driving an automobile a hundred and twenty-eight miles per hour—and he says that we are accelerating. He reminds his audiences that buffalo were shot for their tongues alone, and he says that we still have a buffalo-tongue economy. "We're hooked on growth. We're addicted to it. In my lifetime, man has used more resources than in all previous history. Technology has just begun to happen. They are *mining* water under Arizona. Cotton is subsidized by all that water. Why

80

grow cotton in Arizona? There is no point to this. People in Texas want to divert the Yukon and have it flow to Texas. We are going to fill San Francisco Bay so we can have another Los Angeles in a state that deserves only one. Why grow to the point of repugnance? Aren't we repugnant enough already? In the new subdivisions, everybody can have a redwood of his own. Consolidated Edison has to quadruple by 1990. Then what else have you got besides kilowatts? The United States has six per cent of the world's population and uses sixty per cent of the world's resources, and one per cent of Americans use sixty per cent of that. When one country gets more than its share, it builds tensions. War is waged over resources. Expansion will destroy us. We need an economics of peaceful stability. Instead, we are fishing off Peru, where the grounds are so rich there's enough protein to feed the undernourished of the world, and we bring the fish up here to fatten our cattle and chickens. We want to build a sea-level canal through Central America. The Pacific, which is colder than the Atlantic, is also higher. The Pacific would flow into the Atlantic and could change the climate of the Caribbean. A dam may be built in the Amazon basin that will flood an area the size of Italy. Aswan Dam, by blocking the flow of certain nutrients, has killed off the sardine fisheries of the eastern Mediterranean. There is a human population problem, but if we succeed in interrupting the cycle of photosynthesis we won't have to worry about it. Good breeding can be overdone. How dense can people be?"

More than one of Brower's colleagues—in the Sierra Club,

of which he was for seventeen years executive director, and, more recently, in his two new organizations, Friends of the Earth and the John Muir Institute for Environmental Studies—has compared him to John Brown. Brower approaches sixty, but under his shock of white hair his grin is youthful and engaging. His tone of voice, soft and mournful, somehow concentrates the intensity of his words. He speaks calmly, almost ironically, of "the last scramble for the last breath of air," as if that were something we had all been planning for. "There is DDT in the tissues of penguins in the Antarctic," he says. "Who put the DDT in Antarctica? We did. We put it on fields, and it went into streams, and into fish, and into more fish, and into the penguins. There is pollution we know about and pollution we don't know about. It took fifty-seven years for us to find out that radiation is harmful, twenty-five years to find out that DDT is harmful, twenty years for cyclamates. We're getting somewhere. We have recently found out that polychlorinated biphenyls, a plastic by-product, have spread throughout the global ecosystem. At Hanford, Washington, radioactive atomic waste is stored in steel tanks that will have to be replaced every fifteen years for a thousand years. We haven't done *anything* well for a thousand years, except multiply. An oil leak in Bristol Bay, Alaska, will put the red salmon out of action. Oil exploration off the Grand Banks of Newfoundland will lead to leaks that will someday wreck the fisheries there. We're hooked. We're addicted. We're committing grand larceny against our children. Ours is a chain-letter economy, in which we pick up early handsome dividends and our children find their mailboxes empty. We must shoot down the SST. Sonic booms are unsound. Why build the fourth New York jetport? What about the fifth, the sixth, the seventh jetport? We've got to kick this addiction. It won't work on a finite planet. When rampant growth happens in an individual, we call it cancer."

To put it mildly, there is something evangelical about Brower. His approach is in some ways analogous to the Reverend Dr. Billy Graham's exhortations to sinners to come forward and be saved now because if you go away without making a decision for Christ coronary thrombosis may level you before you reach the exit. Brower's crusade, like Graham's, began many years ago, and Brower's may have been more effective. The clamorous concern now being expressed about conservation issues and environmental problems is an amplification—a delayed echo—of what Brower and others have been saying for decades. Brower is a visionary. He wants—literally—to save the world. He has been an emotionalist in an age of dangerous reason. He thinks that conservation should be "an ethic and conscience in everything we do, whatever our field of endeavor"—in a word, a religion. If religions arise to meet the most severe of human crises, now and then religions may come too late, and that may be the case with this one. In Brower's fight to save air and canyons, to defend wilderness and control the growth of population, he is obviously desperate, an extreme and driven man. His field, being the relationship of everything to everything else and how it is not working, is so comprehensive that no one can comprehend it. Hence the need for

83

a religion and for a visionary to lead it. Brower once said to me, "We are in a kind of religion, an ethic with regard to terrain, and this religion is closest to the Buddhist, I suppose." I have often heard him speak of "drawing people into the religion," and of being able to sense at once when people already have the religion; I also remember a time, on a trail in the Sierra Nevada , when he said, "We can take some cues from other religions. There is something else to do than bang your way forward."

Throughout the sermon, Brower quotes the gospel—the gospel according to John Muir ("When we try to pick out anything by itself, we find it hitched to everything else in the universe"), the gospel according to Henry David Thoreau ("What is the good of a house if you don't have a tolerable planet to put it on?"), the gospel according to Buckminster Fuller ("Technology must do more with less"), and the gospel according to Pogo ("We have met the enemy and he is us"). A great deal of the sermon is, in fact, a chain of one-liners from the thinking sector: "The only true dignity of man is his ability to fight against insurmountable odds" (Ignazio Silone), "Civilization is a thin veneer over what made us what we are" (Sigurd Olson), "Despair is a sin" (C. P. Snow), "Every cause is a lost cause unless we defuse the population bomb" (Paul Ehrlich), "The wilderness holds answers to questions man has not yet learned how to ask" (Nancy Newhall).

Brower has ample ideas of his own about what might be done. He says, "Roughly ninety per cent of the earth has felt man's hand already, sometimes brutally, sometimes

84

gently. Now let's say, 'That's the limit.' We should go back over the ninety and not touch the remaining ten per cent. We should go back, and do better, with ingenuity. Recycle things. Loop the system." When he sees an enormous hole in the ground in the middle of New York City, he says, "That's all right. That's part of the ninety." In non-wilderness areas, he is nowhere happier than in places where the ninety has been imaginatively gone over—for example, Ghirardelli Square in San Francisco, a complex of shops and restaurants in a kind of brick Xanadu that was once a chocolate factory. When someone asks him what one person can do, Brower begins by mentioning Rachel Carson. Then he tells about David Pesonen, a young man in California who stopped a nuclear-power station singlehanded. Then he sprays questions. "Are you willing to pay more for steak, if cattle graze on level ground and not on erodable hills? Are you willing to pay more for electricity, if the power plant doesn't pollute air or water?" He taunts the assembled sinners. "You are villains not to share your apples with worms. Bite the worms. They won't hurt nearly as much as the insecticide does. You are villains if you keep buying automobiles. Leave these monsters in the showroom." Invariably, he includes what must be his favorite slogan: "Fight blight, burn a billboard tonight!"

The cause is, in a sense, hopeless. "Conservationists have to win again and again and again," he says. "The enemy only has to win once. We are not out for ourselves. We can't win. We can only get a stay of execution. That is the best we can hope for. If the dam is not built, the damsite is still there. Blocking something is easiest. Getting a wilderness bill, a Redwoods Park bill, a Cascades Park bill, is toughest of all."

Brower is somewhat inconvenienced by the fact that he is a human being, fated, like everyone else, to use the resources of the earth, to help pollute its air, to jam its population. The sermon becomes confessional when he reveals, as he almost always does, that he has four children and lives in a redwood house. "We all make mistakes," he explains. His own mistakes don't really trouble him, though, for he has his eye on what he knows to be right. After he gave a lecture at Yale once, I asked him where he got the interesting skein of statistics that six per cent of the world's population uses sixty per cent of the world's resources and one per cent of the six per cent uses sixty per cent of the sixty per cent. What resources? Kleenex? The Mesabi Range?

Brower said the figures had been worked out in the head of a friend of his from data assembled "to the best of his recollection."

"To the best of his *recollection?*"

"Yes," Brower said, and assured me that figures in themselves are merely indices. What matters is that they feel right. Brower feels things. He is suspicious of education and frankly distrustful of experts. He has no regard for training per se. His intuition seeks the nature of the man inside the knowledge. His sentiments are incredibly lofty. I once heard him say, "It's pretty easy to revere life if you think of all the things it's done while it was onstage." He is not sombre, though. Reading a newspaper, he will come upon a piece by

86

a conservation writer and say, "I like that. He's neutral the right way."

Brower is a conservationist, but he is not a conservative. I have heard him ask someone, "Do you like the world so much that you want to keep it the way it is?"—an odd question to be coming from David Brower, but he was talking about the world of men. The world of nature is something else. Brower is against the George Washington Bridge. He is against the Golden Gate Bridge. He remembers San Francisco when the bridge was not there, and he says the entrance to the bay was a much more beautiful scene without it. He would like to cut back the population of the United States to a hundred million. He has said that from the point of view of land use the country has not looked right since 1830. There are conservationists (a few, anyway) who are even more vociferous than Brower, but none with his immense reputation, none with his record of battles fought and won—defeater of dams, defender of wilderness. He must be the most unrelenting fighter for conservation in the world. Russell Train, chairman of the President's Council on Environmental Quality, once said, "Thank God for Dave Brower. He makes it so easy for the rest of us to be reasonable. Somebody has to be a little extreme. Dave is a little hairy at times, but you do need somebody riding out there in front."

▲

The office of Charles Fraser, the developer, is in a small building about halfway between an undeveloped jungle and an alligator pond on Hilton Head Island, South Carolina. Alligators sometimes crawl along the sidewalk between the jungle and the pond. The alligators are natives and Fraser is not. Fraser was anxious lest the alligators be disturbed when, in 1957, he began building roads and golf courses and clearing homesites on some five thousand acres of the island, so he fed them great hunks of raw beef to lull them into acceptance of his bulldozers. The alligators swallowed it. They live now in water hazards and other artificial ponds throughout Fraser's Sea Pines Plantation. On his office wall Fraser has a picture of himself, in a white suit and a panama hat, walking an alligator. Signs along the fairways say, "Please do not molest the alligators." Fraser tried something similar with the bald eagles that were there, but the eagles would have none of it, and they flew away.

Fraser is a short man, heavyset, prominent in the forehead, dark curly hair wisping out behind. The first time I saw him, he was standing on a floating dock at his Sea Pines marina, drinking Portuguese rosé and wearing tennis shoes, white trousers, and a blue striped shirt. Those who know him would not instantly recognize such a snapshot, for although Fraser has built one of the creamiest resorts in America, he himself is not the resort type. He drinks little and plays less. Recreation is his business, and business seems to be his recreation. He almost always wears a plain dark suit. He tucks his chin in and sits straight when he is saying something important, and the more important it is, the straighter he sits. He talks about "marketing-acceptance factors" and about how "public money floats better than joint-venture money." His conversation is predominantly about money—its flows, its freezes, its cataracts, its sources, its deltas. He speaks in a clear, authoritative voice, very slowly, as if he were writing a contract as he goes along.

When Fraser first saw Hilton Head Island, rimmed with beaches and the ocean, it was a wilderness of palmettos, live oaks, Sabal palms, egret rookeries, and tupelo swamps shimmering with rattlesnakes and cottonmouths. What he saw there horrified him. Fraser is a visionary. He did not see the rattlesnakes. He saw Coney Island rising from the swamps. He saw what he calls "visual pollution." He saw Myrtle Beach, Asbury Park, Seaside Heights, and Atlantic City. He saw the whole sorry coastline of the Atlantic states—two thousand miles of used flypaper. The flies had missed here and there—Blackbeard Island, Cape Fear, Hilton Head— leaving pristine and visible some segments of one of the longest and most beautiful chains of barrier beaches in the world. Fraser, who was twenty-one, felt that development of some kind was inevitable at Hilton Head, and that it need not look like Myrtle Beach, and need not be done in dissonance with nature. He went to Yale Law School, and the course that most absorbed him was Myres McDougal's Land Use Planning and Allocation by Private Agreement. The gist of what McDougal had to say was that the use of property ought to be planned, because when development is allowed to occur without control the result can be a form of destruction. Throughout his years in New Haven, Fraser was obsessed with a desire to create on Hilton Head Island a resort community over which he would retain absolute aesthetic control, and he was in a position to do so, since his family owned much of the island.

Fraser's father, Lieutenant General Joseph B. Fraser, was a lumber king in Hinesville, Georgia, whenever there was not a war. He and several partners had bought the island for its timber and its speculative potentialities. Charles Fraser worked in summer with the timbering teams and successfully urged that no cutting be done in oceanfront stands of virgin pine. He also drove up and down the coast-line from Virginia Beach to Miami seeking out the original developers of beachfront properties wherever he could find them and asking, "If you had it to do over again, what would you do differently?" From *haut monde* to honky-tonk and back again, they told him what a shortsighted mistake it had been to line up a row of houses along a beach and then put a road just behind the houses, creating a safety hazard and reducing the value of all the lots on the inland side of the road. They told him that large houses have a way of becoming boarding houses. They told him that control is quickly lost if it is not ironclad. Fraser regularly read almost all the journals of architecture. He went to the National Archives, in Washington, and looked up surveyors' notebooks from the eighteen-sixties, because he wanted his development to be of a piece with history, and he tried to locate old cotton fields, wartime fortifications, and vanished Taras. In 1956, with no development experience and not much money, he returned permanently to Hilton Head, where he began to sketch in the air with his hands scenes that he alone could see. Locally, he was considered a major and absolute nut. To his mother he confided, "I may never make any money, but I want to create something beautiful." She told him he was going to waste his time and his legal talent. She says now, "Of course, a person doesn't often have a chance to take wilderness and make something of it. Charles has a sense of beauty and balance. He saw the possibilities there. I think he would have been a painter if he hadn't chosen to do something else."

Sea Pines Plantation appears to be something painted by a single hand, in greens, grays, and browns. Its roads, meandering among the live oaks and Sabal palms, were bent wherever necessary to miss the big trees. All stop signs are green. Private roadside mailboxes are all green. Fireplugs are green. So far there are five hundred and fifty private houses, built by five hundred and fifty individual owners, yet most of the houses have cedar-shake roofs and bleached-cypress siding, the intention being that they should blend into their environment like spotted fawns. Some houses are set back in the woods along the fairways. (There are fifty-four fairways.) Other houses are on narrow drives that lead toward the beach from the principal roads, which are considerably inland. No one in the plantation lacks convenient access to the sea, because Fraser left dozens of fifty-foot public swaths between his arterial roads and the beach, and he has built walkways through the swaths. Neither the beach nor the line of primary dunes behind it has been built upon. Fraser spent fifty thousand dollars to save one live oak when he built a seawall for a harbor he dredged. Trees crowd the roads—dangerously in some places—but Fraser will not remove a tree until automobiles have crashed into it at least twice. He has one section of about a thousand acres that he calls the Main Wildlife Sanctuary and Woodland Recreation Area, and he has legally committed himself to leave twenty-five per cent of the plantation in its natural state. When prospective buyers used to ask about snakes, Fraser would say amelioratively, "Snakes? We'll show you a couple this afternoon." But the snakes eventually received the message, and now they do not show anymore. Alligators are packed up and sent to zoos when they become six feet long. Fraser has a private police force that spends most of its time protecting alligators and deer from poachers. The alligator hides are worth a hundred dollars apiece. Fraser's live oaks were once Methuselan with moss, but after he discovered that rain-soaked Spanish moss can get so heavy it cracks limbs, crews of barbers were sent into the trees to create an overhead garden of Vandykes.

An aerial view of Sea Pines Plantation reveals the great number of houses there, and how close to one another they really are, whereas an observer on the ground—even in the most densely built areas—feels that he is in a partly cleared woodland with some houses blended into it, nothing more. Fraser accomplished this in a region where people have traditionally liked to proclaim their prominence by piling red bricks into enormous cubes and placing before them rows of white columns. He did it—although he occasionally met strong opposition from buyers, bankers, and even subordinates in his own organization—by writing some forty pages of restrictions to attach to every deed. It was a reverse bill of rights (ironclad), a set of ten times ten commandments—take it or leave. The first restriction in the long list gives a suggestion of the whole: it says that any plan or specification can be disallowed by Fraser for any reason whatever. In the early days, when Fraser was operating more on hope than on money (and in full knowledge that half the bankers in South Carolina thought he would soon go under), he was nonetheless so uncompromising that he was ready without hesitation to reject the house plans even of a textile king. If the king refused to conform, Fraser bought back his land. One giddy homeowner tried to paint his house yellow—a historic moment at Sea Pines Plantation—but Fraser backed him down, blending him into the landscape along with his house.

Fraser is cruising through Sea Pines in an air-conditioned green Dodge. A man who is opening a green mailbox marked "H. F. Scheetz, Jr." looks up and waves hello. Fraser lowers the window. "Hi, Henry!" he says as he glides by. Up goes the window. "I operate as nonelected mayor, so I have to act as if I were elected," he explains. "There is democracy of communication here but autocracy of decision-making. Our corporate contracts and deed covenants are the constitution and bylaws of the community. The only way you can have aesthetic control is through the power of ownership. We have more power than a zoning board has. I have centralized the decision-making process, but I'll listen to anybody." The marvel is not whom he listens to but who listens to him. The car passes some of the nation's most authoritative mailboxes—McCormack of Comsat, Hipp of Liberty Life, Taylor of New York State wine, Twining of the Air Force, Simmons of the mattress, Close of Springs Mills. Fraser calls the plantation "a high-quality destination resort," and it has proved to be the destination of a fairly extensive variety of people—not just the barons of war and commerce but also retirees with wan incomes, golfers of most incomes and all handicaps, tennis players of the wider levels, a few painters, a few writers, and rich widows from the North, who bring their late husbands to Fraser's graveyard and then build homes for themselves in the plantation. What these people have in common is Fraser. He is Yahweh. He is not merely the mayor and the zoning board, he is the living ark of the deed covenant. He is the artist who has painted them into the corners he has sold them. A few owners have put sums like two hundred and fifty and three hundred thousand dollars into their houses, but most are in the forty- to fifty-thousand-dollar range, and Fraser has also built condominium villas that sold originally for as little as nineteen thousand—a minimum that has since risen to thirty-eight thousand. He has also built a small town, shops and all, with apartments that rent for two hundred and fifty to three hundred dollars a month. He figures he can blend fifteen hundred more houses into the trees, and one more golf course.

The chairman of the Continental Mortgage Forum recently introduced Fraser as "one of the two finest developers in the United States," not mentioning his peer. Lyndon Johnson appointed him to the Citizens' Advisory Committee on Outdoor Recreation and Natural Beauty. Fraser is also Commissioner of Parks, Recreation, and Tourism for the

South Carolina coast. Now forty-one, he has made twenty million dollars in the past ten years, but he, his friends, and his enemies all agree that personal profit is not paramount among his motives. Fraser's drive seems to have been directed toward accomplishment for its own sake, toward aesthetics for the sake of an aesthetic criterion. Sea Pines has evolved, perhaps, as a kind of monument.

Fraser considers himself a true conservationist, and he will say that he thinks of most so-called conservationists as "preservationists" but that he prefers to call them "druids." "Ancient druids used to sacrifice human beings under oak trees," he says. "Modern druids worship trees and sacrifice human beings to those trees. They want to save things they like, all for themselves." He is aware of the importance of the larger environment. He says he would like to establish a College of the Oceans—"you know, pot, ecology, the whole bag." He reads the newsletter of the Conservation Foundation. He knows the vital position of salt marshes in marine ecology. "Salt marshes are productive feeding grounds for seafood," he says. "In the immediate marsh boundaries of Hilton Head Island, in the marsh flood plain, we save seventy-five per cent of the marsh, as a balanced approach between the interests of recreation and the interests of the druids. Man has to use some of the salt marsh if he is going to live near the sea. A few years ago, anybody would have said it was O.K. to build anything in a salt marsh. Now the society has so much money that we can afford to wonder. The druids get emotional and say you are upsetting ecology if you as much as touch the salt marsh, and you *have* to be polite. But you can't take the position that production of seafood is the most important issue in America. The druids dismiss me as a quote developer unquote, and that makes me mad."

▲

There must be a very remarkable druid at Hammond, Inc., in New York, for Hammond has published a large map that seems particularly notable for what can only be a deliberate omission. It happens that the longest undeveloped beach on the Atlantic coast of the United States forms the eastern shoreline of a very large island, no part of which appears on this map—Hammond's Superior Map of the United States, four feet wide, one inch to seventy miles—although the map shows clearly such islands as Ocracoke, Hatteras, Assateague, Long Beach, and Manhattan, all of which are smaller. The name of the missing island is Cumberland. Virtually uninhabited, it lies off the coast of Georgia. It is the largest and the southernmost of the Georgia sea islands, and on the map the place where Cumberland Island should be is filled with nothing but blue Atlantic, although other sea islands—St. Simons, Sapelo, Ossabaw—stand forth in bold outline to the north. Clearly the work of a druid cartographer.

Cumberland Island, a third larger than Manhattan, has a population of eleven. Its beach is a couple of hundred yards wide and consists of a white sand that is fine and soft to the touch. The beach is just under twenty miles long, and thus, although there are no obstructions whatever, it is impossible to see from one end of it to the other, because the beach itself drops from sight with the curve of the earth. Wild horses, gray and brown, roam the beach, apparently for the sheer pleasure of the salt air. Poachers round them up from time to time and sell them to rodeos for fifteen dollars apiece. Wild pigs seem to like the Cumberland beach, too. The figure of a man is an unusual thing there. New, young dunes rise behind the beach, and behind the dunes are marshes, fresh or tidal. In some of the marshes and in ponds and lakes elsewhere on the island live alligators fourteen feet long. The people of the island will not say specifically where the alligators are. They are fond of their tremendous reptiles. Poachers, commando-fashion, come for them by night, kill them, and take just the hides. Behind the marshes stand the old dunes, high, smooth as talc, sloped precipitously like lines of cresting waves, and covered with pioneer grasses. At the back of the dunes begins a live-oak forest. The canopies of the oaks nearest the beach have been so pruned by the wind that they appear to have been shaped by design in a medieval garden. Among the oaks are slash pines and red cedars—trees also tolerant of salt. Sand-lane roads wind through the forest. Poachers use them in pursuit of white-tailed deer. Hotels in Jacksonville pay thirty-five dollars a deer. Through the woods run thousands of wild pigs. Now and again, a piglet is stopped by a diamondback.

A generally high bluff rims the western shore of the island, and along it are irregular humps—Indian burial mounds that have never been opened. Watched from the bluff, sunsets gradually spread out over a salt marsh five miles wide. This distance from the mainland in part explains why Cumberland Island remains as it is at this apparently late date in the history of the world. There is no bridge. The salt marsh is the most extensive one south of the Chesapeake. It is dominated by cord grass that rises higher than a man's head. The higher the tide, the higher the grass in a tidal marsh, and the Georgia coast has seven-foot tides. An acre of that marsh is ten times as fertile as the most fertile acre in Iowa. Roots of the cord grass reach down into the ooze and mine nutrients. When the grass dies and crumbles, it becomes high-protein detritus. Shrimp spend a part of their life cycle in there eating the crumbled grass. In the marsh, too, is a soup of microscopic plants, of phosphorus, nitrogen, calcium. Oysters grow there. Fish feed in the marshes and on marsh foods washed by the tides. If a quarter acre of marsh could be lifted up and shaken in the air, anchovies would fall out, and crabs, menhaden, croakers, butterfish, flounders, tonguefish, squid. Bigger things eat the things that eat the marsh, and thus the marsh is the broad base of a marine-food pyramid that ultimately breaks the surface to feed the appetite of man.

Tidal creeks penetrate Cumberland Island, and along their edges, when the tide is low, hundreds of thousands of oysters are exposed to view. Shrimp, fast-wiggling and translucent, feed between the beds of oysters. No wonder the Indians wanted to be buried on Cumberland Island. The only wonder is that the island now is much as it was when the Indian mounds were built. It has not always been so. There are stands of virgin pine and virgin live oak on Cumberland, but the island as a whole is a reclaimed wilderness. Orange and olive groves stood there once, and plantations of rice, indigo, and cotton. At the outbreak of the Civil War, the sea islands were abandoned. Later, rich Yankees began competing with one another in the acquisition of Georgia islands, and nearly all of Cumberland was bought by a Carnegie—Andrew's brother Thomas. His family, as it increased, built several enormous houses, and two or three of these are still in fair condition, but the others make Cumberland the world's foremost island in salt-sprayed baronial ruins. The Carnegie heirs are in the third, fourth, and fifth generations, and their number is so large that they went to court not long ago and had the island divided. Conservationists, noting this, and realizing that not all Carnegies could afford to hold land anymore, began to move toward finding a way to keep the island from being developed. They spoke of Cumberland as—in the words of one of Brower's colleagues in the Sierra Club—"a spot in our eyes, a dream that may not come true." Then, in October, 1968, three Carnegies—Tom, Andrew, and Henry—sold three thousand acres of Cumberland Island for one and a half million dollars to Charles E. Fraser.

There was an expression that had been in the air there since the days of the rice and indigo plantations, and now it rose again to currency: "The Devil has his tail wrapped around Cumberland Island."

▲

With "the purchase of lands on Cumberland Island," as Fraser termed the event, the issue was joined for one of the great land-use battles of recent times. Remaining Carnegie heirs closed ranks against him. All over the coast and, in fact, all over the South—particularly in Atlanta, Augusta, Columbia, and Athens (the University of Georgia)—people began talking intensely about Fraser.

"He walked into the Cloister at Sea Island and he said, 'I'm the golden boy of the Golden Isles, and I've just bought three thousand acres of Cumberland Island.' "

"I want to shoot the son of a bitch."

"He is a visionary young man who has learned that conservation can pay."

"No. Charlie is a conservationist in the real sense. He wants to harmonize a modern environment with all the endowments of nature."

"Conservation to Charlie means, in great part, that Charlie should not be bitten by a mosquito."

"He thinks he's a home boy with a lot of clout in Georgia, but he'll find out what he can do with his pink-sock golfers."

"Charles himself is interested in power. That's what motivates him. Everybody thinks he will go into politics."

"He would dearly love to be governor of South Carolina, and he would be fabulous."

"He doesn't have the stomach for it. In politics, there's a lot you can't control. Where he is, he controls everything."

"I'm an ecosystems man. It's not the island alone that interests me. It's the island, the marsh, and the sea. If the marshes are saved, there would not be much ecological loss with development. If you're going to have a developer, I'm all for Fraser. Unplanned development would spoil it."

"I don't think his declared intentions are always his true intentions."

"He's a demon. He has no principles."

"He is a little man walking empty with a cartoon balloon before his mouth, talking and talking as if to create a Charles Fraser who isn't there."

"Fraser says he wants to make these islands available to the people. Horse manure. He means taking it from the old rich and giving it to the new rich. Let's just be straight. A fifty-thousand-dollar investment ain't too many of the people."

"He does things no other developer would. Those concrete bulkheads at Hilton Head cost him three-quarters of a million dollars. He could have had steel for two hundred thousand."

"Steel bulkheads are an eyesore."

"Mr. Fraser does preserve environment. The university hopes that most of Cumberland can become a National Seashore, so people can enjoy it. It can't be all wilderness. We think it should be a mix—people in nature."

"The guy is tearing off an island just as if it were a postage stamp. He's behaving like a hunter knocking off buffaloes. We'll challenge anyone who wants to be the Buffalo Bill of the Georgia coast."

"He has half-baked, two-bit ideas. He's thinking very

small. I challenge Charlie Baby to come up with something exciting. We are going to come into an age when people want more than a bag of sticks and some white balls."

"We can't afford to think in Colonial land-grab terminology anymore. We could set a precedent on Cumberland Island for recreational land use in America. Let's do something imaginative. Fraser's plans are not big enough. The golf-course bit should go to the mainland. There could be three planned communities on the mainland, with Cumberland their open space."

"You come in to the coast slowly. It grows on you. River mouths, marshes, tidal creeks, islands, the continental shelf, and the continental slope are really an integral unit, a single system. We have had integration of the races in the sixties, and we are going to have integration of man and the land in the seventies, or we'll all be gone in the eighties."

▲

On a cold but sunlit November day, a small airplane, giving up altitude, flew down the west shore of Cumberland, banked left, crossed the island, and moved out to sea. Sitting side by side behind the pilot were Brower and Fraser. The plane turned, still descending, and went in low over the water and low over the wind-pruned live oaks and down into a clearing, where the ground was so rough that the landing gear thumped like drumfire. A man in khaki trousers and a wild-boarskin shirt waited at the edge of the woods. The aircraft wheeled around at the far end of the clearing and taxied back toward him through waist-high fennel.

Fraser and Brower had met only the evening before, at Hilton Head, and Fraser, in his direct way, had begun their relationship by giving Brower a dry Martini and then telling him what a conservationist is. Fraser said, "I call anyone a druid who prefers trees to people. A conservationist too often is just a preservationist, and a preservationist is a druid. I think of land use in terms of people. At Hilton Head, we have proved that you can take any natural area and make it available to people while at the same time preserving its beauty." Brower listened and, for the moment, said nothing. He had not expected so young a man. Fraser's dynamism impressed him, and so did Sea Pines Plantation. Fraser, for his part, was surprised by what he took to be, in Brower, an absence of thorns. Expecting an angry Zeus, he found instead someone who appeared to be "unargumentative, quiet, and shy."

Now, on Cumberland Island, the pilot cut the props, and into the resulting serenity stepped Fraser and Brower. Fraser wore a duck hunter's jacket and twill trousers that were faced with heavy canvas. Brower had on an old blue sweater, gray trousers, and white basketball shoes. The name of the man in the boarskin shirt was Sam Candler. Hands were shaken all around. Brower said it was "nice to be aboard the island." The weather was discussed. Amiability was the keynote.

Candler, who was thirty-eight, had spent much of his life

on the island. He grew up on its oysters and shrimp. His children were doing the same. Candler knew where the alligators were, and he had a boxful of diamondback rattles, from snakes he had killed with a hackberry stick. Notches on the stick corresponded to rattles in the box, and Candler would have dearly loved to be able to make an additional notch that corresponded to Charles E. Fraser. There was native gentility in Candler, however, and he did not permit his darker sentiments to surface in the presence of his new neighbor. Candler spoke even more softly than Brower did, and the accents of Atlanta were in his voice. He was a slim man of medium height, with dark hair. He owned, with others in his family, the part of Cumberland Island that Thomas Carnegie did not buy. The Candler property, about twenty-two hundred acres at the north end, was the site of a rambling wooden inn (now Candler's house) in which business flourished around the turn of the century but atrophied after causeways were built to other islands. Candler's great-grandfather was the pharmacist who developed and wholly owned the Coca-Cola Company; his son, Candler's grandfather, bought the Cumberland property in 1928.

The pilot said goodbye. The airplane waddled into position and took off.

"An airport is essential here," Fraser said.

"But it's not a nice neighbor," Brower told him.

"Yes, but ours would be just large enough for small private jets, no more," Fraser said. "Let's go see Cumberland Oaks."

Cumberland Oaks was Fraser's working title for the development he intended to build on Cumberland Island. To get to the site, we drove about ten miles on narrow sand-lane roads, Fraser at the wheel of a Land Rover that belonged to his company. Sunlight came down in slivers through the moss in the canopies of huge virgin oaks. We stopped near one, and Brower paced the ground under it. The limbs reached out so far that, bent by their own weight, they plowed into the ground, from which they emerged farther out, leafily. Yucca grew in a crotch twenty feet high. Brower computed that the canopy covered fifteen thousand square feet of ground.

We drove on, through long stretches that were straight to the end of perspective. "This is a vast island," Fraser said. "It can absorb dozens of different kinds of uses. You won't even be able to *find* the uses, it's so vast—if it is handled with discretion." Brower was silent. "By going into islands, I tarnish my shining image, because I irritate so many druids," Fraser said. Brower smiled. The Land Rover raced along at forty miles per hour and occasionally bounced over a corduroy bridge. Eventually Fraser said, with both humor and sarcasm in his voice, "Now we're on my property. Don't it look lovely?" Brower said sincerely that lovely was how it looked, with its palmettos, its live oaks, its slash and longleaf pines. To Fraser, it was obviously raw and incomplete, but even now he could clearly see before his eyes finished villas and finished roads. So complete was this vision, in fact, that Fraser turned off the existing road and began to zip through the trees, rounding imaginary corners and hugging subdivisional curves. Spiky palmettos rattled against the Land Rover's sides like venetian blinds. Pine branches smacked against the windshield, making explosive noises and causing us all, instinctively, to blink and cover our heads with our arms. A buck and two does leaped away from the oncoming vehicle, and Candler, raising his voice above the din, commented pointedly that on an island heavy with deer they were the first we had seen. "Variety of wildlife increases sharply with variety of food," Fraser said, accelerating. "A place like Sea Pines Plantation has more wildlife than an untouched forest—more browsing, more habitat variation."

The western edge of Fraser's property was a high bluff over the Cumberland River, a tidal lagoon separating the island from the broad marsh, and as we stood there looking down at the water and across to the distant mainland Fraser said, "We'll have slides here, so kids can slide down the bluff."

"You could have swings here on these cedars," Brower offered.

Fraser said that some of the cedars on his property had been planted by Scottish soldiers who had built and manned a stockade there in the early eighteenth century. Development was thus nothing new around Cumberland Oaks. Looking west across the water and the marsh, he confided that he was envisioning a seven-hundred-and-fifty-thousand-dollar system of towers, cables, and aerial gondolas to carry people to Cumberland Oaks from the mainland. "Brunswick Pulp & Paper owns those forests over there," Fraser said. "I would describe Brunswick Pulp & Paper as 'friendly.'"

Wild grapevines as thick as hawsers hung from the high limbs of Fraser's pines, and as we moved east through the woods Brower found them irresistible. Fraser stopped the Land Rover so Brower could get out and swing on one—fifty feet in an arc through the air. He crashed into a palmetto.

Between the deep woods and the beach, among the secondary dunes of Cumberland Oaks, was a freshwater lake—Whitney Lake—so clear and lustrous that it gave Fraser's property a slight edge over all other parts of the island. Set in all the whiteness of the big hills of powder sand, the lake was so blue that day it paled the blue sky. Near the north end of the lake, three skeletal trees protruded from the slopes of sand—branches intact, but spare and dead. A buzzard sat in each tree. The trees were dead because the dunes were marching. Slowly, these enormous hills, shaped and reshaped by the wind, were moving south. They had already filled up half of Fraser's lake, and, left alone, they would eventually fill it all. Five buzzards stood at the edge of the water. Fraser stood there, too, with the unconcealed look on his face of a man watching a major asset disappear. "We've got to stabilize these dunes," he said.

Brower, for his part, was moved by the lyricism of the scene. If destruction is natural, Brower is for it. "I think it's just fine to see it happen," he said.

Fraser said, "I've got to restore dune-grass vegetation here. I've got to put the lake back to its original size. I'm an advocate of lakes."

"There's a place for development and there's a place for nature," said Candler.

"What would you move the dunes with?" I asked Fraser.

"Spoons, hoes, shovels—earthmoving equipment. You change natural gradings very cheaply with a bulldozer," he said.

Fraser went on to tell us that the lake had been named for Eli Whitney. Planters on the island had given Whitney financial support toward the development of the cotton gin. "This lake shouldn't be allowed to disappear," Fraser said. "There should be canoes on it for children. Children should be fishing here for bream. There is nothing here now but buzzards and dead trees."

Thinking of his three thousand acres as a whole, I asked him privately what he would like to build there by Whitney Lake.

"Houses!" he whispered.

The northernmost tip of the ocean beach was a long spit owned by Candler. We drove up there, inadvertently filling the sky with sandpipers and gulls. Then we turned and, in the late-afternoon light, went south all the way. The big beach ran on and on before us, white and dazzling in the clear sunlight. No other human beings were there. Of the several houses on Cumberland Island, the one nearest to the beach was a half mile back in the woods. We had been driving for a while when Candler remarked that we were nearing the end of his property. He has two and a half miles of beach. He said, "The only thing wrong with this beach—the traffic's so bad." Shells crunched under the wheels and salt foam flew out behind us. Plastic jugs, light bulbs, bottles, and buoys had drifted up along the scum line, but nowhere near enough of them to defeat the wild beach. I remembered the shoreline of the Hudson River at Barrytown, New York. A photographer from *Sports Illustrated* had caught up with Brower near there, and they had gone to some difficulty to get down to the river's edge, so that Brower could be photographed with the wind tousling his white hair against a background of natural beauty. For the occasion, Brower had changed from a topcoat into a ski parka, and the picture was successful—this ecological Isaiah by the wide water. It was just a head-and-shoulders shot, so it did not include the immediate environment of Brower's feet. The shore of the Hudson River, a hundred miles upstream from Manhattan, was literally obscured by aerosol cans, plastic bottles, boat cushions, sheets of polyethylene, bricks, industrial scum, globs of asphalt, and a tattered yacht flag. Now, on the Cumberland beach, Fraser, for the moment, was sounding much like a hard-line real-estate man. He was saying that we had beside us "the finest, gentlest breakers on the Atlantic coast." Brower said that where he came from such ripples were not called breakers. We got out of the Land Rover and walked for a while. Brower paused and studied the reflection of the falling sun on the surfaces of the breakers. This was what mattered to him—the play of light. He saw a horseshoe crab and had no idea what it was. He picked up a whelk shell and a clamshell and asked the names of the creatures that had lived in them. He wondered what made the holes of fiddler crabs. Shrimp boats were working offshore. Brower said he liked the look of them, bristling with spars. Brower seems to think in scenes. He seems to paint them in his mind's eye, and in these scenes not everything made by man is unacceptable. Shrimp boats on a bobbing sea are O.K. On the waterfront in San Francisco, he and I once drove at dusk past a big schooner that is perennially moored there, and its high rigging was beautiful in the fading light. "There should be more masts against the sky," Brower said. And now, back in the Land Rover, he looked up at high cumulus that was assembling over the ocean and he spoke of "sky mountains," while Fraser looked the other way and said that the primary dunes were in a process of severe disintegration, and the Land Rover moved on at forty miles per hour, crunching Paisley-spotted shells of the tiger crab.

"Have you ever been on a shrimp boat to see how they work?" Brower said.

"I have—when I was twelve," said Fraser. "I want a shrimp boat out of Cumberland Oaks, taking four or five kids a day."

The distance was so great across the beach and the dunes to the woods that I asked Fraser how far back he thought the nearest of his houses ought to be.

"The mainland," said Candler.

"That's a real dilemma here," Fraser said. "If the houses are set back in the trees, it's bad for recreation. What we need is an extensive tree-planting program to build up destroyed areas by the shore."

"Destroyed?"

"Destroyed. These dunes are not ordinary."

"They have always looked all right to me," Candler said.

"Pine trees grow exceedingly fast down by the ocean," Fraser went on.

Brower was silent.

"Within thirty years, there need to be fifty thousand more points for a week's visit on the Georgia coast," Fraser said. "You don't decrease the number of Americans taking a vacation by sealing off a particular land area. Surveys show that seventy-five per cent of Americans prefer beaches to all other places of recreation. I believe in human enjoyment of beaches, but, of course, the druids think it would be a shame and a crime to have people on this beach—a shame and a crime."

Acres of ducks darkened the swells of the ocean. A wild brown mare and her gray colt stood ankle-deep in a tidal pool. "Sam, why didn't you buy the property I bought?" Fraser said.

"I didn't have enough money," Candler said.

A line of pelicans—nineteen of them—flew south just seaward of the breakers. Pelicans fly single file, and Candler said he could remember them going by in lines a hundred pelicans long. That was in an era that seems to be gone. DDT has got into the bodies of pelicans and eventually into the shells of their eggs, and its effect on the shells is that they come out so thin they crack before chicks are ready to be born. Brower remarked that the pelican is one of the earth's oldest species. He quoted Robinson Jeffers, saying that pelicans "remember the cone that the oldest redwood dropped from." We were nearing the end of the beach, and we could see Florida across the mouth of the St. Mary's River. The pelicans kept going, like flying boxcars, across the river. "They're doomed," Brower said. "Maybe we're lined up behind those pelicans."

▲

Fraser is descended from the Frasers of Inverness and the Bacons of Dorchester, who began their existence in the New World as Puritans of seventeenth-century New England and gradually moved in a southerly direction, establishing Dorchester, Massachusetts; Dorchester, South Carolina; and, eventually, Dorchester, Georgia. The Bacons and the Frasers were on the original roll of the Midway Church Settlement, a seat of Presbyterian enlightenment important in the history of Georgia and the South. The Frasers regularly sent their sons to Edinburgh to be educated. The 1810 census showed the Frasers to be among the ten foremost slave-holders in the state. One distinguished Fraser voted against secession, and another used a slingshot against troops of General Sherman. For two hundred years, the family has had what Fraser calls "substantial amounts of land," and the family's "social antennae" (as he would phrase it) have developed a length and sensitivity commensurate with the family's history and standing. Consequently, nothing makes Fraser sit straighter and tuck his chin in deeper than the assertion—often repeated in gossip—that his acquisition of property on Cumberland Island was something straight out of Chekhov: the capitulation of a fine old family under inexorable pressure from a *nouveau-riche* developer.

Having returned to the middle of the island, Fraser stopped at a small graveyard, not by chance. Its walls were made of tabby—lime, sand, and oyster shells—and it was only twenty feet square. Dusk had come and was now heavy, and Brower grew rhapsodic about the penumbral grays, the deep shafts of varied gloom under the high trees. Fraser, meanwhile, was intently pointing to a stone, and there was still enough light to reveal what was written there: "Thomas Morrison Carnegie, born Dunfermline, 1843, died Pittsburgh, 1886." What Fraser wanted us to note was that the Carnegies are comparatively recent immigrants. He referred to them as "upstarts," and said, "I have no patience with them. They have no sense of history. They think the history of the island is the history of their occupancy. They think history began when they arrived. Look there." He was pointing to another stone. The inscription said, "In memory of Catherine Miller, widow of Major General Nathaniel Greene, Commander-in-Chief of the American Revolutionary Army in the Southern Department, 1783, who died November 2, 1814, aged 59 years. She possessed great talents and exalted virtues." "More talents and more virtues than all the Carnegies put together," Fraser said. "Her friend General Lighthorse Harry Lee died here on Cumberland Island. Did you know that, Sam?"

"Yes, I did, Charles."

"The family of my friend Brailsford Nightingale, in Savannah, owned parts of this island when the Carnegies were still herding sheep. The Nightingales have been elegant for more generations than you can count. They are descendants of General Greene. They had subdivided this island and were going to make it a rich man's retreat before the Carnegies had ever heard of it, but the Nightingales were thwarted by history. Reconstruction was a brutal wipeout. And now the Carnegie druids do not wish to share the island with other people. They think only Carnegie eyes are sensitive enough to appreciate the beauties of that beach out there. On any list of America's hundred most selfish families these poor new-rich Carnegies must be placed very high."

On the way in from the beach we had passed another kind of graveyard—a place where at least twenty automobiles and pickup trucks were disintegrating in flakes of rust. It was this scene that had set off Fraser's ridicule and fulminating scorn. Here, he said, was a family posing as conservationists, attempting at this very moment to enlist the support of the federal government in protecting their island with them on it, and this junk heap was their idea of preserving natural beauty. He said he would like to bring a bulldozer to the island and cover the junk up. And he said, "How about your place, Sam? You must have some things up there that need covering up. Could I give you a neighborly hand?"

"I have nothing to hide," Candler said.

"You haven't got anything one day with a bulldozer won't cure."

Fraser's relationship with the Carnegies had not always been as clearly defined as it now appeared to be. The Carnegie heirs were a diffuse group. Most of them spent little or no time on the island. Two or three of them lived there. During early negotiations, the Carnegies' attitudes toward Fraser varied considerably. Then a social event framed the nature of things to come. A few days after Fraser was given the deed to his new lands, one of the Carnegie heirs, a pretty girl in her twenties, was married on Cumberland Island. The groom, a junior executive in Fraser's Sea Pines Plantation Company, had been assigned to the Cumberland Island project and had met his bride there. That should be plot enough for a Deep South Lorca, but there was more: The bride was the author of a Sierra Club book. Fraser arrived for the wedding, as various Carnegies recall the scene, wearing an ascot and carrying an enormous leather map case. They say that he unstrapped his case in the middle of the reception and displayed plats and plans for his new utopia on Cumberland Island. They say he called them idiots not to understand the concept of conservation easements. Moreover, they say, he burped in front of ladies. According to the bride, Fraser "galvanized the Carnegies into unanimity." They united in order to block Fraser in any way possible, most notably by promoting a Cumberland Island National Seashore, with "inholding" or "life-time-estate" provisions for established residents. The groom, for his part, defected. He quit the Sea Pines Plantation Company, the better to live happily ever after.

And now, by the little graveyard, in the near-darkness,

115

Fraser said to Candler, "Sam, what do you think of that line about the hundred most selfish families? Do you think I can get some mileage out of that? Shall I hone it?"

Candler said, "You don't want to develop that line, Charles. You might spoil it."

"All right, I'll leave it as it is, but did you know that one of the older Carnegie ladies told Stewart Udall that only blooded heirs of Thomas and Lucy Carnegie should ever be allowed to set foot on this island?"

"How do you know that?"

"I was told by someone present. She wagged her finger under Udall's nose and said, 'Only blooded heirs of Thomas and Lucy Carnegie should ever set foot on Cumberland Island.' You know, during all the present talk about National Parks and National Seashores the Carnegies have been keeping something under the table. A few years ago, most of them were in favor of strip-mining the beach. The sand is full of ilmenite, zirconium, and rutile. I have no patience with the Carnegies. All they want to do is maximize their dollar, either through the mining industry or through the federal government or by piggybacking on me. Now look at one more headstone."

The inscription said, "Thomas Hutchison, Golf Professional, eldest son of William and Helen H. of St. Andrews, Scotland. Born October 6, 1877. Died December 8, 1900."

"He was surely the first golf pro to be buried in America," Fraser said. "When this property was bought by the Carnegies, there were no golf courses in the United States. A golf club had once been in operation in Charleston and another in Savannah, but they had long since ceased. The oldest

116

continuing golf organization in the United States is St. Andrews of Yonkers. It was built in 1888, and from then to 1900 golf swept the country. Hundreds of courses were built, including one here on Cumberland Island—where we landed in the airplane. The Carnegies brought this young man from St. Andrews, Scotland, and he died here when he was twenty-three."

Fraser had already made something out of his research into the history of golf in the South. He had arranged with the Professional Golfers Association a new hundred-thousand-dollar tournament, to be held at Sea Pines, and to be called the Heritage Classic, because the first golf club in America had been built in South Carolina. The first Heritage Classic was won by Arnold Palmer, and because Palmer had not won a tournament in more than a year this was major news in the sporting world, and the names of Sea Pines and Hilton Head were publicized throughout the United States. As we stood there in the graveyard on Cumberland Island, I looked at the tombstone and then at Fraser, feeling a kind of awe for his luck. Someday, if he had his way, there would surely be a hundred-thousand-dollar First Pro Classic on the Thomas Hutchison Memorial Golf Course, Cumberland Oaks.

Reflectively, Fraser placed a hand on the tombstone and said, "Druids hate golf. I keep telling them golf was here seventy-five years ago. Dave, you wouldn't mind if I built a little golf course here on Cumberland Island, would you?"

"I suppose not, if you don't take too many trees," Brower said.

"You know I don't take too many trees, Dave," Fraser

said. He turned to Candler. "Sam, Dave is going to let us have a golf club here."

"He is?"

"Yes."

"That's damned white of him."

▲

That night, in a place called Greyfield, before a big fireplace that glowed with burning logs and coals of oak, Fraser and Brower spread out on the floor a map of Cumberland Island twelve feet long. Together they crawled around on it, pushing cocktails from one part of the island to another. Antlers hung above them, and portraits of Carnegies, and a portrait of George Washington, while the skull of a loggerhead turtle, huge and primordially human—or so it seemed—faced them from a cluttered shelf. The map was about twenty years old and bore the names of quick and dead Carnegies —Thomas M. Carnegie, Jr., Florence Carnegie Perkins, Carter C. B. Carnegie, Lucy Ricketson Ferguson, Nancy Carnegie Johnston, Andrew Carnegie II. Greyfield, with high porch and high columns and a need of paint, belonged to Lucy Ferguson's son Rick, who once ran a plastics factory in Jacksonville and was now running Greyfield as an inn for selected guests. Fraser could hardly be said to have been selected, but he was made welcome at Greyfield, and nearly all the inimical things said about him were said behind his back. Meanwhile, on his hands and knees on the big map, a Martini at his fingertips, Brower was saying, "When you get onto a floor with a big map, something happens. You think you're in an airplane."

Fraser said to Brower, "Dave, suppose you owned this island. Suppose you were the dictator and were under no financial pressure whatever. How do you think this island ought to be used in the last thirty years of this century?"

Brower said, "I'd have one feeder point to the beach per mile."

Fraser seemed to levitate, to float above the map. He might have been a skin diver who had just picked up a doubloon. The excitement he felt was almost, but not quite, palpable. Was this the David Brower of Friends of the Earth and the Sierra Club—the slayer of environmental dragons, the uncompromising defender of wilderness? Fraser's face was a mask. He tucked in his chin and said unflickeringly, "I call them 'beach social points.'"

The conversation was semi-private. Several duck hunters and the odd Carnegie or two moved around it. Beyond the firelit room was a long hall, and off this was a small room where Rick Ferguson had set up a self-service bar. He was there, a short man, wiry and strong, in tennis shoes, khaki trousers, an old blue oxford-cloth button-down shirt—the great-grandson of Thomas Carnegie. Ferguson's wife, in a long hostess gown, was with him.

"Cumberland Island is going down the drain," Ferguson said.

"Fraser's drain," said his wife.

"I feel like a man who has just been told his block is up for urban renewal. We seem to be on the sidelines while this big show is going on. All I want to protect here is my children's inheritance."

"We have no rights except what the majority lets us do."

"I was giving Charles the benefit of the doubt once when I called him insensitive. I think his rudeness is an inherent characteristic."

"Charles is over-self-righteous. He thinks he is absolutely right and is doing good—and that is his mistake."

"No one is interested in this island but the family, basically."

Ferguson excused himself and went off to slice a roast of beef.

On the floor in the big room, Brower was leaning on his elbows. Fraser was on his knees.

"How many people would you, as dictator, permit on the island July 4, 1980?" Fraser asked.

"I don't know," Brower said. "An answer is needed, but if on the evening I come here I come up with an answer, I'm an ass."

"Ninety per cent of Americans want bedrooms when they are on vacation," Fraser went on. "Ten per cent want to camp with automobiles. Only five per cent of that ten per cent—or five people in a thousand—want wilderness camping. How many would you permit on this island, and how would you accommodate them?"

"Let's keep Cumberland Island for the five per cent of the ten per cent who want wilderness," Sam Candler said.

"I think I'd recommend the Yosemite formula," Brower

said. "Seven square miles of Yosemite bears heavy and concentrated use. The rest is open."

Brower has deep affection for the Yosemite, which is, or was once, the most beautiful valley in the Sierra Nevada. He has spent whole years there, and a great deal of time in or around the valley throughout his life. When he is in the Yosemite, he seems to be packed in nostalgia, and he appears to be unaffected by the valley's peeled-log Levittowns, its tent cities, its bumper-to-bumper traffic, and its newsstands—all results of what has been described as the fatal beauty of Yosemite. In all likelihood, he accepts Yosemite whole because the valley was already urbanized when he was young. And now, on Cumberland Island, he was recommending something similar. "I would cluster all development in one place," he said to Fraser. "People could walk elsewhere. Walking on the beach is the most important thing a person can do here. If you were going to develop just one spot on the entire island, where would that be?"

"To be very explicit, my tract has tremendous diversity," Fraser said. "I have Whitney Lake, the Scotch fort, the marching dunes. But we're pretending *you're* the dictator. The island as a whole is twenty miles long. How many people can your area of concentration absorb?"

"You mean at night?"

"Yes, at night."

"They do have to be there at night," Brower mused. "People will want to see what the sky is saying. It's their last contact with Mother Earth."

121

"How many people?" Fraser said again.

"It's their last chance to listen to the sun and the moon."

"How many people?"

Brower shrugged. He said, finally, "I wouldn't mind having a population of twenty thousand here."

"Twenty thousand?"

"Twenty thousand."

Brower got up and went in to make himself another drink. When he came back, he and Fraser agreed that if a National Park or Seashore could surround Fraser's place on Cumberland Island, that would be very good. Brower said that what worried him was that if Fraser were to go ahead and develop his land without some such federal protection of the rest of the island, the value of the remaining properties would rise so sharply that the neighbors might have to let the land go to less capable developers. Fraser said that worried him, too.

"Whatever happens to this island, the automobile should be ruled out," Brower went on.

"I agree," said Fraser.

"No tourist vehicles. No bridge. No private automobiles or other vehicles on the beach."

"I agree."

"How would you get people around?"

"Perhaps jeep trains."

"How would you bring in food and services?"

"In sky vans—mini flying boxcars."

"Whatever you do, don't give the island to Detroit. Zermatt is carless. Stehekin, in the State of Washington, is car-

less. It is good conservation practice, if you are going to develop, to concentrate people and leave wild land around
them. People need earning territory—territory they have to
earn by walking, limping, crawling, or whatever they can
do. With that around them, the concentrated area is important, and I wouldn't mind so many people. Not at all. When
you get out of the city, you hear the planet talk, and here it
is talking. If the dunes want to march, they ought to march.
I know how you feel, but the land itself should not be controlled."

"The Brower Plan is economically sound," Fraser said. "I
could live within the constraints imposed by the Brower
dictatorship. As the island is now, birds enjoy it but nobody's swimming here. Nobody's in the woods. There are no
people. The island's stable population is eleven. That comes
to one person per mile and three-quarters of beach."

Rick Ferguson had come into the room to say the roast
beef was ready. "One person per mile and three-quarters of
beach is just about right," he said.

"Why do you think the family have kept it this way?"
said Mrs. Ferguson. "Because they *feel* so strongly."

"If you can keep it the way it is, fine," Brower told her.
"But I don't think that is one of your choices."

▲

Not long after Fraser acquired his property on Cumberland
Island, he established a public campsite there. He admitted
privately that he had several motives. For one thing, it was

123

a way to acquaint the public with the island. For another, it would set a precedent for public use of the island at a fee. Finally, and most ingeniously, it would put Stewart Udall in a position where he might have to criticize camping—for Udall had been employed by the Carnegies as a conservation consultant, or, as Fraser insisted on putting it, as "a hired mudslinger." Udall said of Fraser, "I want to push Charlie into a corner where he has to face the truth. He is good news as a developer and bad news for Cumberland Island. He is not interested in having a reputation as a spoiler, but he can't have it both ways. He tries to incorporate conservation with economic development, but it doesn't work."

One motive Fraser emphatically did not have for establishing his campsite was a desire to camp on Cumberland Island himself. Fraser is not in any sense a woodsman or a man of the outdoors, as he will acknowledge without shame. Nonetheless, under urging from Brower and from me, he had agreed to sleep in his own campsite. And now, after dinner at Greyfield, the three of us went out into the black, cold night and headed for the campsite, which Brower was eager to see. After we had gone some distance through the woods, Fraser said, "I'm most happy to go along with this, but, frankly, you are taking me out of my element."

It would be difficult to say whose element the campsite was. It consisted of fifteen so-called recreation vehicles— tent-covered, two-wheeled automobile trailers, with electric lights, electric heat, and four-burner gas stoves. A central toilet facility had hot showers, an ice machine, and a cedar-shake roof in the Sea Pines manner. Fraser said he believed in "use," and that this was a good way to start. He said he planned to build a small store at the campsite and, eventually, to rent jeeps by the day. Meanwhile, he was charging five dollars a night for the mobile tents—loss leaders if ever there were any, for they cost him fifteen hundred dollars apiece.

Two of the vehicles had been set up for us, and they faced each other, like canvas tourist cabins, across an area filled with palmettos and cast-iron grills that were mounted on galvanized pipes. Brower went into one tent and Fraser and I into the other. While we were unrolling our sleeping bags, Fraser said, "Very interesting, his views. They're so different from what I thought they would be." Spreading out the contents of a briefcase on a Formica-topped table, Fraser looked through them. Then he got out a pen and began to read and make marginalia. He read an article in the *Yale Law Journal* on large-lot zoning; he read a piece from the Beirut *Daily Star* on a new kind of sewage-disposal system; and in an issue of *American Forests* he read something called "The Destiny of Conservation Depends Upon Truth." "At the moment, I am rather aggravated about the distruth of statements made by certain druids," he commented. "But Dave is not a druid—not the way he was talking. Arthur D. Little would get ninety thousand dollars for the consultancy Dave did tonight." For morning, Fraser set aside a copy of *Audubon* magazine, a book called *Land, People, and Policy*, and the first draft of a prospectus for the first public issue of stock in his company. He shut off the light. "The highest and best use of this island is for chil-

125

dren," he said as he was settling to sleep. "I believe, however, that the struggle here is too complicated, and therefore hopeless, and that no reasonable development will ever go on here."

Brower called out from across the palmettos, "Good night, and sleep well if your conscience is good."

Fraser called back, "My conscience is always bad, and I always sleep very well. Good night."

"Good night."

▲

Sleep was not all that easy, in part because the bunks folded out and were cantilevered from either end of the mobile unit. Fraser and I were balanced on a kind of rubber-tired seesaw. Every time he rolled to his right, I went up a little, and every time he rolled to his left I went down. I lay there long into the night thinking mainly about the peculiar pattern of the relationship developing between him and Brower.

A beach is for children, Fraser had said. I didn't think he was just groping for a key to a bank vault. I had seen swings of various kinds all over Sea Pines Plantation—swings hanging from the eaves of covered walkways, swings hanging from the limbs of trees. He had bought tricycles and scattered them around. He had strung hammocks at the height of children. Walking among the fresh foundations of his new town, he had once said to me, "Landscape architects won't hang swings. They say swings are not a strong enough de-sign statement. I'll wait until the landscape architects are fin-ished, and then I'll hang a hundred swings from the live oaks. I'll have a vender selling watermelon, too—roasted oysters in the winter, ice-cold slices of watermelon in the summer." Fraser and his wife, Mary, lived in a glass-and-cy-press Sea Pines house. Gardeners took care of the environ-ment. The Frasers had two daughters, aged four and two. The Frasers believed that the direction of a life was estab-lished almost at the beginning—that no years were as telling as the earliest ones. Hence, among other things, the Montes-sori School (where Mary Fraser worked) and the swings all over the plantation.

Brower was reverent toward the young. His faith had told him that the young would do better with the earth. He did not associate lumber companies, motor companies, chemical companies, or mining companies with youth. He admired Young Turks while he attacked Old Philistines. By his ready admission, he had learned a great deal from his own chil-dren, all of whom were college age or older. Brower himself looked almost unnaturally young, his white hair notwith-standing. He sometimes seemed to trust young people's judgment over his own. He often said, "I'm impressed with what young people can do before older people tell them it's impossible." Any number of times since we had come to Cumberland Island, he had commented on the youth of Charles Fraser. "I didn't know he was so young. . . . What energy! I didn't expect so young a man."

Out through a picket fence and down a deeply shaded

street Fraser, as a boy, had walked every day to school. He was blond then, and had curly hair. His mother and father used to buy athletic equipment for him, but he would give it all away and sit on the porch reading books while his friends—endangering the camellias—played football or baseball on his family's lawn. His family owned nearly half of Hinesville. Their house had been the first in Liberty County to have running water, inside toilets, and two pianos. The land for the First Presbyterian Church had been a gift from his grandmother. His father had been moderator of the Presbyterian Church of the State of Georgia and president of the Men of the Presbyterian Church of the United States of America. The church was the Frasers' locus of being. "Holy, holy, holy," Fraser had chanted one day at Hilton Head, waving his hands like a choir leader as he revealed these credentials. "As a Calvinist, I was told that you're not supposed to do all the pleasurable things in life. But eventually I realized that I would be part of the elect no matter what sins I might commit." He said that at the age of thirteen he had been a newspaper entrepreneur. Under his ironclad managerial control, his entire Boy Scout troop sold papers. He fished the creeks, hunted squirrels, collected buckeyes. He became the first Eagle Scout in the history of Liberty County. Now the executives of the Sea Pines Plantation Company included a high proportion of former Eagle Scouts. On the Sea Pines boardroom wall was a life-size portrait of Fraser's father, in uniform, and beside this portrait stood two flags—a United States flag and the three-star flag of a lieutenant general. General Fraser commanded the first ground troops to land on New Guinea. He went into France with Patton. Charles Fraser, at the age of ten, had been quite relieved when his father's unit was converted from cavalry to anti-aircraft. Charles hated horses and did not want to ride them. His interests were elsewhere. In becoming an Eagle Scout, he won merit badges in birds, reptiles, conservation. He loved beautiful objects and had a gift for design. He painted his family's coat of arms on a mug, applying the paint with toothpicks. His brother, Joe, was an athlete. Liberty was a coastal county, and one thing Charles particularly liked to do was to go to the beaches and build castles in the sand.

Fraser's mother-in-law, before she became that, used to send newspaper clippings about him and his plantation to her daughter wherever she might be—at Stephens College, in Columbia, Missouri, for example, or, later, in Washington, D.C., where she worked for Senator Thurmond. "Mary's mother is a very sensible Southern mother, who knows that her daughter's standard of living depends on her husband's income," Fraser once explained. "Mary was accustomed to a very elegant standard. She had a Cadillac to drive to school when she was sixteen—and that was just the leftover car around the place." Mary, in her college days, had not so much as met him. He was twelve years older than she, and he lived two hundred miles from Greenville, her home town. Nonetheless, she dutifully read and saved the clippings. Eventually, she would more or less save Fraser. Small details not being his forte, she had assumed responsibility for looking after them. He forgot everything

—his money, his briefcase, his topcoat, his whereabouts. He lost every hat he ever owned. "Hats are a nuisance and an absurdity," he complained. He was not absentminded, his wife decided. He was simply not interested in petty detail. He read all the time. He read walking upstairs, he read until his food was cold, and he rigged up extra lights in the car so he could read while she drove. He forgot his raincoat but remembered facts. Three minutes after he walked into a room, it was a shambles. "Have you read this? What did you think of it? What do you think about that?" Newspapers hit the floor. Sixteen books came off the shelves. "Charles says there is so little time, and never a convenient time for anything, so if you want to do something you have to just do it," Mary once said. "He applies this to a trip to Europe, to conceiving a child—to anything." Mary, dark-haired, dark-eyed, slender, was collaterally descended from a family named Lawton that once grew cotton on Hilton Head Island—in fact, on the site of Sea Pines Plantation. When Fraser's archival researches yielded this fragment, he was most pleased. He and Mary began to refer to it as "the heritage." He would talk about it with a detached grin, but he was obviously happy that he had something like that to be detached about. "The Lawtons were planters," he liked to say, invoking images of antebellum wealth and antebellum elegance. He once introduced his four-year-old daughter, Laura Lawton, to a stranger.

"Hello, Laura," said the stranger.

"It will have to be Laura Lawton, I'm afraid," said Fraser.

"Laura Lawton, say 'My great-great-great-great-great-granddaddy planted cotton here.'"

In an office at the University of California Press, in 1941, Anne Hus had demonstrated to David Brower that she could lean over and pick a newspaper off the floor with her teeth. She wondered if he could do the same. They shared the office. Both were editors, working on what she called "rewarmed dissertations with the scaffolding taken out." He said stiffly, about the newspaper stunt, that one does not do that sort of thing in an office, and he refused to try. Brower as an editor made her jealous. "He was so much better than I. I have never understood where he got his feel for words. He is a great editor. He liberates what is good in an author's work. It just infuriates me that anyone who has read so little can do that. I have been reading since I was four. He has never read anything. He hasn't read novels. He knows very little about English literature. Yet he has a remarkable sense of language." Anne had been born in Oakland. Her father was a man who failed at so many jobs that he said he should go into undertaking in order to prolong human life. Her grandfather John P. Irish, editor and politician, was the man who was debating with William Jennings Bryan when Bryan said, "You shall not crucify mankind upon a cross of gold." Brower was in the 10th Mountain Division when, in 1943, he proposed to Anne by mail. Before he went overseas, they lived in Colorado for a time, and then in West Virginia, where Brower taught climbing to the mountain troops, on the Seneca Rocks. He spent so much time on bivouac that she despaired and went to Washington, where she edited combat narratives for Army Intelligence. Later, she went back to the University of California. She was still an editor there when I met her, in 1969. A gentle person, she seemed almost complacent—an impression that belied her sharpness of ear and eye. I remembered her telling him once, "I never see people I'd rather be married to than you —especially in National Parks." Brower obviously needed her guidance. Away from her, he could scarcely pass a phone booth without getting into it and calling her. At the Press, in their early days, he had dropped from sight now and again and gone off to the Sierra Nevada. After he had been doing this for a while, she told him he was getting away with murder. Leaning over, he picked a newspaper off the floor with his teeth and said he had to practice some-where. He asked her to go with him to the mountains. She loved the sea and didn't like the mountains. "Edna Ferber said mountains were beautiful but dumb, and that is how I felt, too. Finally, I went on a Sierra Club trip just to fill in. To get through it, I took a bottle, and took nips. After three days, I really loved the trip—such incredible country. Until you've seen him up there, you don't know him."

I thought of Brower in the Sierra Nevada, in the Valley of the Mineral King. To conservationists, the Mineral King had become an Agincourt, a Saratoga, an El Alamein. Walt Disney Productions wanted to string the slopes with lifts and build enough hotels there to draw a million people a year. Mineral King had been mentioned as an excellent setting for the Winter Olympics of 1976, celebrating the two-hundredth anniversary of the birth of the nation. Brower and I went to Mineral King together. My impression was that—all other considerations aside—it was an extraordinarily good site for a skiing resort. A stream ran through the middle of the valley, and if you stood beside it and looked up and around you saw eleven conical peaks, the points of a granite coronet. The steep slopes of these mountains were covered with red fir, juniper, aspen, and foxtail pine. Great rising swaths were treeless and meadowed. Hannes Schneider had called it the best potential ski area in California. So much snow had been there the winter before that avalanches had sheared off many hundreds of trees twenty feet above the ground—the snow was that deep. The avalanches had been so powerful that they had not stopped at the bottom of the valley but had climbed the other side, smashing trees. In the geological history of the Sierra Nevada, Mineral King was an old valley. The Sierra Nevada had been a minor mountain range of about four thousand feet when it began the great upheaval that made it higher than the Rockies. New streams cut through the new uplift and created valleys like the Yosemite, with wide, flat floors and sheer walls. The Mineral King was lifted with the mountains and remained intact, a V-shaped valley—alpine, ancestral—and it caught snow like nothing else in a mountain range that was named for the snow that fell there. Brower had done a ski survey of Mineral King once, long ago, and had said that he favored limited development. He said now that he essentially felt the same way. Sitting under a big cottonwood with his feet in the stream, he pointed out that the valley was, for one thing, not wilderness. A road reached into it. A couple of dozen buildings were there, a sawmill, and corrals belonging to a pack station. Listening to him, a surprised conservationist might have thought that the Antichrist had come to the Mineral King disguised as David Brower. But to the Disney interests Brower would not have seemed like much of an advocate. Looking around at the Mineral King peaks, he decided that although he was for limited development, he was against ski lifts. He said he preferred to see people earn their ski runs by climbing with skins attached to their skis. Moreover, he was against improvement of the existing access road, an incredibly twisting cliff-hanger so narrow and serpentine that a million people trying to use it would grow old before they reached the valley. Brower said Disney Productions should build a hundred-million-dollar tunnel, or fly people in—save the approaching mountains, hang the cost. Told he was being almost poetically impractical, Brower responded that the Disney people were going to change something forever, so they could amortize the changes over a thousand years.

Fraser rolled over and sighed in his sleep. I wondered if in the day to follow he would find that Brower's apparent tolerance for the development of Cumberland Island was equally tied in string. He sighed again. Possibly he was dreaming of Badische Anilin-& Soda-Fabrik Aktiengesellschaft, a name, of all names, that haunted him. Fraser was hoist on a most ironic petard. Badische Anilin-& Soda-Fabrik Aktiengesellschaft, known as BASF, was a company that made, among other things, petrochemicals and dyes for the textile and furniture industries, and not long before they had decided to expand beyond Ludwigshafen and into the American South. They searched in several states for a site for a new plant. There were plenty of possibilities. What in the end attracted the Germans most in all the South was Sea Pines Plantation. German chemical kings apparently liked golf and the good life, too. They had found a plant site on Victoria Bluff, three miles from Hilton Head Island. Air and water pollution would surely follow. Fraser, meanwhile, had become the unlikely leader of a battalion of druids, whose war cry was "BASF—Bad Air, Sick Fish!" Ultimately, Fraser and his druids would drive the Germans away, but he had learned that even in the beauty of Sea Pines Plantation there could be something fatal.

▲

One night of camping out, even in a fifteen-hundred-dollar mobile tent, was quite enough for Fraser, and the following evening we transferred our gear to a motorship called the *Intrepid*, which had slipped quietly down the coast from Hilton Head and into the Cumberland River. The size of Fraser's yacht was proportionate to his distaste for wilderness. The yacht was ninety feet long. It contained five staterooms and a floor-through saloon. Its bar was stocked with Tanqueray gin. Fraser's Southern antennae had reached out unobtrusively, suprasocially, and their research had shown that Tanqueray is Brower's gin of gins. With the moral support of a friendly doctor, Brower once used gin as his principal weapon in humbling a stomach ulcer, and he was so successful that he has ever since been a friend of the preventive Martini. With something beatific in his eyes, he ritually asks for "a Martini with Tanqueray gin, straight up, with nothing in it." Lemon, he feels, changes the taste, while only a madman would accept an olive, for an olive displaces two cubic centimetres of gin. It had been a long, full day on the island, and Brower now settled back with a drink innocent of additives and watched the sun fall behind the Georgia mainland. Fraser sipped bourbon and Calvinistically worked on his stock prospectus—for several hundred thousand shares of something he was calling Recreational Environments, Inc., at twenty-five dollars a share. He needed money for expansion—not only to Cumberland Island but to half a dozen other places he was interested in, from North Carolina to Hawaii. He had just bought six miles of beautiful and undeveloped white beach under coconut palms on the east coast of Puerto Rico, and only the week before he had gone as far as Kuwait looking for funds. "I'm just an oyster catcher from South Carolina begging for money," he said, moving a blue pencil over the prospectus. "A million dollars. A million dollars. Can you spare a million dollars?"

"Look at that sun on that smog!" Brower said. Shining low through the air over the paper-mill country, the sun tended to embarrass Georgia. It appeared to be setting in black-bean gumbo. "American industry never asked my permission to shorten my life," Brower went on. "They have taken two years off my life and will take seven years off my

136

children's. These are figures I can't support, but I believe them."

"Let's put a paper mill over here on Cumberland Island and get the smell away from the cities," Fraser said, looking at Sam Candler, who went on looking at the sunset.

"Whatever their economy is, they haven't paid for the people's air," Brower said. "They should be given six months to clean up or go out of business. Roll, you earth. I swear the sunset is slower than the sunrise."

On the beach at six-fifty-seven that morning, we had watched the sun jump into the clear sea air like a rubber ball released from a hand below the ocean's surface. Fraser, over breakfast, read an article called "The Dying Marsh" in *Audubon* magazine, and throughout the day he pelted Brower with sachets and nosegays. Hurtling along a narrow, curving sand road through the forest, Fraser said, "We'll call this the David Brower Scenic Drive." And later, approaching an attractive swamp, he said, "We'll call this the David Brower Wildlife Sanctuary and Woodland Recreation Area." In a small skiff on a tidal creek, Fraser stood in the bow like George Washington and spoke what were apparently the first words of a press release he was forming in his mind: "Charles Fraser announced today the results of a detailed study for the use of Cumberland Island." Sam Candler had one hand on the skiff's tiller and with the other he was bailing. Flights of ducks passed overhead. The tide was low. Using a small anchor as a kind of oyster rake, Fraser knocked hundreds of oysters loose from an exposed bed. He

137

was clearly feeling very good. On the beach, he drove at fifty-five miles an hour and said gleefully that he had decided to name his new development the Cumberland Island Conservation Association.

Brower was feeling good, too—obviously enjoying himself on the island. Why he did not rise up and clout Fraser, verbally, seemed a little odd to me, but I had seen him before in situations where he was getting the sense and feel of something, and while his mind was working toward a settled attitude he had vacillated or lapsed into an uncharacteristic passivity. In the North Cascades, he had known where he was. He had been there before, and had fought for the wilderness there. He had never before set foot on Cumberland Island. Fraser, ebullient, was finding Brower so docile that he wouldn't even call him a druid, and in a sense Fraser was right, for the rote behavior of an ordinary member of the priesthood should be simple to predict. This, however, was—as Fraser apparently did not grasp—no ordinary member of the priesthood. This was the inscrutable lord of the forest, the sacramentarian of *ecologia americana,* the Archdruid himself. Fraser's difficulties with druids were anything but over.

Lacking a target in the invisible Brower, Fraser eventually attacked Candler. Candler, whose original intention had been merely to help show Brower around the island, had tried to hold off from saying much, but now there was a gun-fusillade argument.

"Sam, you just don't want people on this beach, do you?" Fraser said.

"I didn't say that," Candler said.

"A man has no more right to personal private property on a beach than he has to a highway, an Army camp, a railroad, a school, a hospital, an airport, a valley to be flooded for a dam. A fundamental part of the pursuit of happiness is one's annual vacation. Hence this beach is for a public purpose."

"Your purpose. I'm happy to have people use the island now, if they make the effort to get over here and to enjoy it."

We happened to be at the southern boundary of Fraser's proposed development. Fraser said that a National Seashore should begin just there and extend all the way to the southern tip of the island—about fifteen miles—and that the north end, above his property, should become "an environmental-protection zone." The development, he promised, would include nothing that would pollute the environment.

"What *would* it have?" Candler asked.

"Houses, a marina, an airport, a store."

"That is not my idea of conservation."

"Tell me, Sam, which Carnegies will break ranks and sell out next?"

No answer.

"How many Carnegies will rub their hands with glee when prices go up because of development?"

No answer.

"Those snobs—high on the list of the hundred most selfish families."

"I'd like to make a list of island destroyers," Candler said.

Fraser said, "The government has a perfect right to condemn my land here if it thinks its use is wiser than mine."

It emerged that a Cumberland Island Conservation Association already existed.

"Name all organizations that exist on the island," Fraser said.

"What do you mean?" Candler asked him.

"Every time I pick up a paper, I read about another organization."

"You mean like your Cumberland Island Holding Company?"

"Name another one."

"The Cumberland Island Conservation Association is the only one I know about," Candler said.

"Is it incorporated?"

"I believe so."

"You *believe* so?"

"Yes."

"Who is the president of the Cumberland Island Conservation Association?"

"I am."

"Is it incorporated?"

"I'm not real sure."

"The light is nice on the water there," Brower said. "The light is getting good."

Brower and Fraser climbed a high dune. Candler stayed on the beach. From the dune, he appeared a lonely figure—the only person on twenty miles of white sand. "People develop passionate attachments to these islands, and any change from the way they have known them since childhood is emotionally disturbing to them," Fraser said. "It's a jolt to them to have any of their property used by strangers."

One afternoon in Atlanta, Candler had told me what Cumberland Island meant to him. "Changes come slowly there, and leave marks on one another," he said. "There is a blending from one era to the next. Indian mounds are there. When I am on Cumberland Island, I see the same things the Indians saw. I would like to live where the Indians lived. They were closer to the earth, a part of the environment. Fraser said that after the hurricane there were no sea oats on Cumberland. The island teaches you the value of patience. The sea oats came back. Dunes that are washed down will return. You've got to have some places that are hard to get to. I don't think this is a selfish thought. I think it's thoughtful."

Fraser, for his part, had told me that nothing would please him more than to develop his property in consonance with a National Seashore that would take up the rest of the island. In fact, he would be hesitant—even unlikely—to develop his land without knowing what might happen around it. Another Sea Pines freshly rising among the live oaks could so enhance the value of the island as a whole that the Carnegies and Candler might find irresistible the offers of ticktack developers. There was so much of Cumberland that, even for a man of Fraser's resources, protective buying was out of the question. So he dreamed of a beautiful enclave in various shades of income, with forever-protected wildernesses stretching away from either side and rationed quantities of the public wandering the great beach.

Now, on the dune, Brower and Fraser—Columbus and Cortez—stood high above the wild and pristine seascape. Fraser said, "I think it is wise public policy for the government to take a place like this from private owners. Don't you agree?"

"Yes."

Candler, who had moved farther down the beach, was an even smaller figure. From the dune, he could be framed between a thumb and forefinger a quarter inch apart. His hands were in his pockets.

"I would like to reverse my ninety-ten here," Brower said. "I would like to see ten per cent developed here and ninety not."

Fraser said, "I hope that can be arranged."

▲

Oysters on the half shell, when they are as fresh as the ones we ate for lunch that day, are so shining and translucent, so nearly transparent, that if you were to drop one on a printed page you could read words through the oyster. I had lived beside tidal creeks at various times in the past, and had once set up my own amateur oyster farm, from which I regularly removed a hundred and forty-four oysters each day to eat before lunch, but even the memory of my oyster farm was turned slightly opaque by the quality of the oysters from Candler's tidal creek. Mantle to palpi, each vitrescent blob was a textural wonder. We ate at least five hundred of them, raw or roasted (over an oak fire)—*Ostrea virginica*, better than the best oysters of Bordeaux, and, as it happened, long-range appetizers to the roasted game hens that were spread before us that evening on Fraser's yacht.

On the yacht, Brower held up his glass and studied the prismatic coupling of gin and light. He then looked off into the rouge afterglow over the marshes to the west. "The outdoor life is all right," he said. "But don't knock the amenities." Pale wines escorted the game hens, and brotherhood bobbed on the water with the yacht, while the dark mass of Cumberland Island stood beside the boat with what Joseph Conrad once described as "the stillness of an implacable force brooding over an inscrutable intention." No one was looking at the island. On a color-television set inside the yacht, the San Francisco 49ers were bombing the Baltimore Colts. Brower said, "Long live the instant playback—the nicest thing technology has given us!"

"We will create a conservation conference center here on the island," Fraser said.

"That will require an airport," said Brower. "I'm Machiavellian enough to know that if you are going to have a conference center you have to have a way to get there."

"We'll let druids land free," Fraser said. "If you were dictator, what would you do with that marsh?"

"Save it! Save the greenery! I can make noise, but you can make deeds," Brower said. "Save the marsh! Grasses are one of the nicest ways the green thing works. The green giant is chlorophyll, really. When I come back in another life, I am going to spend my whole life in grasses. I'm addicted to the entire planet. I don't want to leave it. I want to get down into it. I want to say hello. On the beach, I could have stopped all day long and looked at those damned shells, looked for all the messages that come not in bottles but in shells. Life began Tuesday noon, and the beautiful organic wholeness of it developed over the next four days. At three minutes before midnight, man appeared. At one-fourth of a second before midnight, Christ arrived. At one-fortieth of a second before midnight, the Industrial Revolution began. You, Charles Fraser, have got to persuade the whole God-damned movement of realtors to have a different kind of responsibility to man than they have. If they don't, God will say that man should be thrown away as an experiment that didn't work. I have seen evidence of what you can do. Now make others do it. The system must be used to reform the system."

Fraser had been listening with his hands clasped behind his head. When Brower finished, Fraser said nothing and sipped his wine.

▲

In the early morning, in the yacht's saloon, Brower performed his matins. He spilled out and sorted the contents of his briefcase—an old and thick one, jammed with books, notebooks, magazines, clippings—and he read for an hour or so, as if to put himself in context. He read a Sierra Club tract called *Machiasport: Oil and the Maine Coast*. He read a copy of a letter from Earl Bell, the planner, to Senator Henry M. Jackson, asking how the island Amchitka could still be called a National Wildlife Refuge since it had become a military missile dump, a military garbage dump, and a site for atomic testing. Simultaneously, Brower made cryptic notes for a talk he would give at Harvard: "Loop the system . . . Ravisher of the Month . . . SST . . . Signs . . . Dams . . . Sawlogs." Reading on, he piled up newsclips on the table before him: "JOIN POLLUTION FIGHT, NATO TOLD," "BP OIL ESTIMATES ALASKA TRACT AT FIVE BILLION BARRELS," "DROWNING AN ECOLOGICAL PARADISE," "CAN ANYONE RUN A CITY?," "PLANNER URGES TWO-CHILD LIMIT," "SLOW DOWN THE OIL RUSH," "BAN ON ABORTION STRUCK DOWN," "THE MAZE OF HAZE THAT SPOILS OUR DAYS," "WE ARE SUBVERSIVES IN THE STATE OF NATURE," "NORTHWEST PASSAGE TO WHAT?" He had heretical material, too: "ALARMISTS IGNORE THE FACTS," "MAN MUST CONTROL NATURE," "THE POPULATION FIRECRACKER" (William Buckley arguing that there is no population explosion), and an editorial from the *New Scientist* mocking the excessive excitability and the platitudes and dogmas of "ecological high priests." Brower next examined a dummy for a conservation newsletter to be called the *National Hammer,* an article from the *Stanford Law Review* called "The SST: From Watts to Harlem in Two Hours," and a list of proposals—to him as publisher—for a series of Suppose We Didn't books, on things that would be best left undeveloped: the SST, the oil refinery in Machiasport, the Alaska pipeline, the sea-level canal through Central America. He read the Leopold Report ("Land drainage . . . will destroy inexorably the South Florida ecosystem") and an article from *Trial* called "Can Law Reclaim Man's Environment?" Finally, he read a piece on architectural ravages in New York City's West Village, and he waved in the air a *Business Week* article—"The War That Business Must Win"—and said, "Here is the first faint streak of dawn coming up over the business world. They are at last finding out that environment is not only to sell."

From below, Fraser appeared, dressed in a dark suit and tie. After breakfast, he was going to leave Cumberland Island in order to do battle with druids in other parts of the South. The rest of us would stay on for a while. Fraser clearly felt that Cumberland was safe, for the moment. In the Land Rover, he drove to the primitive airstrip. The same small plane was waiting in the field of fennel. Fraser walked confidently away from an atmosphere of cordial farewells and climbed into the plane. The pilot advanced the engines to maximum r.p.m. Four wild horses slowly walked off the runway. The plane raced through the fennel and into the air. Watching it rise and turn, Brower said softly, "What makes Sammy run in the South?"

We got into Candler's jeep and spent the day slowly reviewing the island. At Candler's speed—ten to twenty miles per hour—details came into focus that, at Fraser's speed, had previously tended to blur. The jeep, for one thing, was open, and we felt the island around us in a way that we had not in Fraser's Land Rover, which was closed in. "You can't see the whole island anyway—it's too big—so you might as well enjoy what you can see," said Candler. "Going along in

Fraser's Land Rover was like going over Niagara Falls in a barrel."

"I've never run into anybody quite like that," Brower said.

"Are you sorry or glad that he developed Hilton Head Island?"

"I don't know. I think probably I'm not glad. I'd rather have more wilderness on the coast than there is. But if it had to be developed, I'm glad it was developed by him."

As we moved along, deer walked across the road in front of us. Candler showed us a place where he had often found arrowheads at low tide and a place where we picked wild grapefruit. We went to the south end of the island, which was ribbed with hummocks and was full of freshwater ponds and tall magnolias. A jetty there had been built ninety years ago at what was then the southernmost point of the island. The jetty was now at least two thousand feet inland from the southern shore. Land had simultaneously been eroding from the north end. Cumberland Island was gradually migrating to Florida, and had already crossed the state line. A sonic boom hit us with a report so loud that Brower staggered as if he had been shot, and tens of thousands of birds—oyster catchers, pelicans, sandpipers, gulls— rose screaming into the air between the Cumberland shore and the Florida mainland. They stayed up there, flapping in panic, for ten minutes, clouds and clouds of shrieking birds. Candler showed us where he had once dug into a mound and found a skeleton in a sitting position, and he told us how as a boy he used to play with muzzled alligators. We

147

visited a tame buzzard at Lucy Ferguson's place, where a rusting automobile engine hung from a tree and no one but the buzzard was home. The buzzard's eyes glittered like the running lights of an airplane. The buzzard nibbled at Brower's basketball shoes. Brower stroked the bird and talked gently to it. The buzzard nibbled at his fingers and draped a talon over his hand. We saw blue herons, bluebills, and egrets in the marshes, and cacti hanging like strings of sausages from live oaks in the woods. At Candler's place, we ate a foot-high pile of shrimp from the tidal creek—under a big kitchen clock on which red lettering said, "Things Go Better With Coke." Shrimp, like oysters, are as transparent as clear gelatine when they come out of the creek. On the beach, Candler noticed the remains of a leatherback turtle, its back as large as a steamer trunk. It had been there for days, but we, whipping by, had not seen it before. We saw wild pigs in the tidal marshes eating seafood, and a flight of seventy cormorants, in imprecise formation, passing overhead.

"What are they trying to spell to us?" Brower said.

"Pepsi-Cola," said Candler.

As far as I could see, though, the message in the sky over Cumberland Island was "Finis." We drove up a marching dune and snowplowed down the other side, leaving fresh tracks in the powdery white sand. The wind would cover them. But how many tracks could the wind cover? Since early morning—in fact, for three days—we had roamed an island bigger than Manhattan and had seen no one on its beach and, except at Candler's place and Greyfield, no one in its interior woodlands. In the late twentieth century, in this part of the world, such an experience was unbelievable. The island was a beautiful and fragile anachronism. We were, as Candler had said, seeing what the Indians saw, and it was not at all difficult to understand why he wanted to "live where the Indians lived . . . closer to the earth, a part of the environment." We, too, had eaten from the tidal creeks and had gone where and how we pleased—a privilege made possible in our time by private ownership. That was the irony of Cumberland Island and the index of its fate. The island was worth nothing when the Muskhogean Creeks lived and fished there. Now it was worth at least ten million dollars, a figure that could swell beyond recognition. Need, temptation, and realistic taxes would eventually wrest the island from its present owners. They would not be able to afford it. The question whether it was right for a few individuals to own twenty miles of beach had already been bypassed by these inexorable facts of economics.

Actually, the resolution was to arrive swiftly. In months to come, druids in massed phalanx were to create so many pressures—social, political, financial—and so much ecological propaganda that Fraser would give up his Cumberland territory, selling Cumberland Oaks to the National Park Foundation. Money for the purchase was to be made available to the Park Service by the Andrew Mellon Foundation, with enough left over to acquire the rest of the island from the other owners. Thus Fraser, in his coming and going, was in the end to be the catalyst that converted Cumberland Island from a private enclave to a national reserve. The other

149

owners, as Brower had said, were without choice, really. They would have preferred to keep the island the way it was—and no wonder. It was Earth in something close to its original state. The alternatives—private development, public park—came nowhere near that, and never would. In the battle for Cumberland Island, there could be human winners here or there, but—no matter what might happen—there could be no victory for Cumberland Island. The Frasers of the world might create their blended landscapes, the Park Service its Yosemites. Either way, or both ways, no one was ever to be as free on that wild beach in the future as we had been that day.

PART 3

A River

Floyd Elgin Dominy raises beef cattle in the Shenandoah Valley. Observed there, hand on a fence, his eyes surveying his pastures, he does not look particularly Virginian. Of middle height, thickset, somewhat bandy-legged, he appears to have been lifted off a horse with block and tackle. He wears bluejeans, a white-and-black striped shirt, and leather boots with heels two inches high. His belt buckle is silver and could not be covered over with a playing card. He wears a string tie that is secured with a piece of petrified dinosaur bone. On his head is a white Stetson.

Thirty-five years ago, Dominy was a county agent in the rangelands of northeastern Wyoming. He could not have come to his job there at a worse time. The Great Drought and the Great Depression had coincided, and the people of the county were destitute. They were not hungry—they could shoot antelope and deer—but they were destitute. Their livestock, with black tongues and protruding ribs, were dying because of lack of water. Dominy, as the agent not only of Campbell County but of the federal government, was empowered to pay eight dollars a head for these cattle —many thousands of them—that were all but decaying where they stood. He paid the eight dollars and shot the cattle.

Dominy was born on a farm in central Nebraska, and all through his youth his family and the families around them talked mainly of the vital weather. They lived close to the hundredth meridian, where, in a sense more fundamental than anything resulting from the events of United States history, the West begins. East of the hundredth meridian, there is enough rain to support agriculture, and west of it there generally is not. The Homestead Act of 1862, in all its promise, did not take into account this ineluctable fact. East of the hundredth meridian, homesteaders on their hundred and sixty acres of land were usually able to fulfill the dream that had been legislated for them. To the west, the odds against them were high. With local exceptions, there just was not enough water. The whole region between the hundredth meridian and the Rocky Mountains was at that time known as the Great American Desert. Still beyond the imagination were the ultramontane basins where almost no rain fell at all.

Growing up on a farm that had been homesteaded by his

grandfather in the eighteen-seventies, Dominy often enough saw talent and energy going to waste under clear skies. The situation was marginal. In some years, more than twenty inches of rain would fall and harvests would be copious. In others, when the figure went below ten, the family lived with the lament that there was no money to buy clothes, or even sufficient food. These radical uncertainties were eventually removed by groundwater development, or reclamation—the storage of what water there was, for use in irrigation. When Dominy was eighteen years old, a big thing to do on a Sunday was to get into the Ford, which had a rumble seat, and go out and see the new dam. In his photo album he put pictures of reservoirs and irrigation projects. ("It was impressive to a dry-land farmer like me to see all that water going down a ditch toward a farm.") Eventually, he came to feel that there would be, in a sense, no West at all were it not for reclamation.

In Campbell County, Wyoming, the situation was not even marginal. This was high, dry country, suitable only for free-ranging livestock, not for farming. In the best of years, only about fourteen inches of rain might fall. "Streams ran water when the snow melted. Otherwise, the gulches were dry. It was the county with the most towns and the fewest people, the most rivers with the least water, and the most cows with the least milk in the world." It was, to the eye, a wide, expansive landscape with beguiling patterns of perspective. Its unending buttes, flat or nippled, were spaced out to the horizons like stone chessmen. Deer and antelope moved among them in herds, and on certain hill-

155

tops cairns marked the graves of men who had hunted buf-falo. The herbage was so thin that forty acres of range could reasonably support only one grazing cow. Nonetheless, the territory had been homesteaded, and the homesteaders sim-ply had not received from the federal government enough land for enough cattle to give them financial equilibrium as ranchers, or from the sky enough water to give them a chance as farmers. They were going backward three steps for each two forward. Then the drought came.

"Nature is a pretty cruel animal. I watched the people there—I mean good folk, industrious, hardworking, frugal—compete with the rigors of nature against hopeless odds. They would ruin their health and still fail." Without waiting for approval from Cheyenne or Washington, the young county agent took it upon himself to overcome nature if the farmers and ranchers could not. He began up near Recluse, on the ranch of a family named Oedekoven, in a small bowl of land where an intermittent stream occasionally flowed. With a four-horse Fresno—an ancestral bulldozer—he moved earth and plugged the crease in the terrain where the water would ordinarily run out and disappear into the ground and the air. He built his little plug in the classic form of the earth-fill dam—a three-for-one slope on the water side and two-for-one the other way. More cattle died, but a pond slowly filled, storing water. The pond is still there, and so is Oedekoven, the rancher.

For two and a half years, Dominy lived with his wife and infant daughter in a stone dugout about three miles outside Gillette, the county seat. For light they used a gasoline lantern. For heat and cooking they had a coal-burning stove. Dominy dug the coal himself out of a hillside. His wife washed clothes on a board. On winter mornings when the temperature was around forty below zero, he made a torch with a rag and a stick, soaked it in kerosene, lighted it, and put it under his car. When the car was warm enough to move, Dominy went off to tell ranchers and farmers about the Corn-Hog Program ("Henry Wallace slaughtering piglets to raise the price of ham"), the Wheat Program (acreage control), or how to build a dam. "Campbell County was my kingdom. When I was twenty-four years old, I was king of the God-damned county." He visited Soda Well, Wild Cat, Teckla, Turnercrest—single-family post offices widely spaced—or he followed the farmers and ranchers into the county seat of the county seat, Jew Jake's Saloon, where there was a poker game that never stopped and where the heads of moose, deer, elk, antelope, and bighorn sheep looked down on him and his subjects, feet on the rail at 9 A.M. Dominy had his first legitimate drink there. The old brass rail is gone—and so is Dominy—but the saloon looks just the same now, and the boys are still there at 9 A.M.

There was an orange scoria butte behind Dominy's place and an alfalfa field in front of it. Rattlesnakes by the clan came out of the butte in the spring, slithered around Dominy's house, and moved on into the alfalfa for the summer. In September, the snakes headed back toward the butte. Tomatoes were ripe in Dominy's garden, and whenever he picked some he first took a hoe and cleared out the rattlesnakes under the vines. Ranchers got up at four in the morning, and sometimes Dominy was outside honking his horn to wake them. He wanted them to come out and build dams—dams, dams, dams. "I had the whole county stirred up. We were moving! Stockpond dam and reservoir sites were supposed to be inspected first by Forest Service rangers, but who knows when they would have come? I took it upon myself to ignore these pettifogging minutiae." Changing the face of the range, he polka-dotted it with ponds. Dominy and the ranchers and farmers built a thousand dams in one year, and when they were finished there wasn't a thirsty cow from Jew Jake's Saloon to the Montana border. "Christ, we did more in that county in one year than any other county in the country. That range program really put me on the national scene."

▲

In the view of conservationists, there is something special about dams, something—as conservation problems go—that is disproportionately and metaphysically sinister. The outermost circle of the Devil's world seems to be a moat filled mainly with DDT. Next to it is a moat of burning gasoline. Within that is a ring of pinheads each covered with a million people—and so on past phalanxed bulldozers and bicuspid chain saws into the absolute epicenter of Hell on earth, where stands a dam. The implications of the dam exceed its true level in the scale of environmental catastrophes. Conservationists who can hold themselves in reasonable check before new oil spills and fresh megalopolises mysteriously go insane at even the thought of a dam. The conservation movement is a mystical and religious force, and possibly the reaction to dams is so violent because rivers are the ultimate metaphors of existence, and dams destroy rivers. Humiliating nature, a dam is evil—placed and solid.

"I hate all dams, large and small," David Brower informs an audience.

A voice from the back of the room asks, "Why are you conservationists always against things?"

"If you are against something, you are for something," Brower answers. "If you are against a dam, you are for a river."

When Brower was a small boy in Berkeley, he used to build dams in Strawberry Creek, on the campus of the University of California, piling up stones in arcs convex to the current, backing up reservoir pools. Then he would kick the dams apart and watch the floods that returned Strawberry Creek to its free-flowing natural state. When Brower was born—in 1912—there was in the Sierra Nevada a valley called Hetch Hetchy that paralleled in shape, size, and beauty the Valley of the Yosemite. The two valleys lay side by side. Both were in Yosemite National Park, which had been established in 1890. Yet within three decades—the National Park notwithstanding—the outlet of Hetch Hetchy was filled with a dam and the entire valley was deeply flooded. Brower was a boy when the dam was being built. He remembers spending his sixth birthday in the hills below Hetch Hetchy and hearing stories of the battle that had been fought over it, a battle that centered on the very definition of conservation. Should it mean preservation of wilderness or wise and varied use of land? John Muir, preservationist, founder of the young Sierra Club, had lost this bitter and, as it happened, final struggle of his life. It had been a battle that split the Sierra Club in two. Fifty-five years later, the Sierra Club would again divide within itself, and the outcome of the resulting battle would force the resignation of its executive director, David Brower, whose unsurprising countermove would be to form a new organization and name it for John Muir.

Not long after Brower's departure from the Sierra Club and his founding of the John Muir Institute, I went to Hetch Hetchy with him and walked along the narrow top of the dam, looking far down one side at the Tuolumne River, emerging like a hose jet from the tailrace, and in the other direction out across the clear blue surface of the reservoir, with its high granite sides—imagining the lost Yosemite below. The scene was bizarre and ironic, or so it seemed to me. Just a short distance across the peaks to the south of us was the Yosemite itself, filled to disaster with cars and people, tens of thousands of people, while here was the Yosemite's natural twin, filled with water. Things were so still at Hetch Hetchy that a wildcat walked insolently across the road near the dam and didn't even look around as he moved on into the woods. And Brower—fifty-six years old and unshakably the most powerful voice in the conservation movement in his country—walked the quiet dam. "It was not needed when it was built, and it is not needed now," he

160

said. "I would like to see it taken down, and watch the process of recovery."

During the years when Brower was developing as a conservationist, many of his most specific and dramatic personal accomplishments had to do with proposed dams. Down the tiers of the Western states, there are any number of excellent damsites that still contain free-flowing rivers because of David Brower—most notably in the immense, arid watershed of the Colorado. Anyone interested, for whatever reason, in the study of water in the West will in the end concentrate on the Colorado, wildest of rivers, foaming, raging, rushing southward—erratic, headlong, incongruous in the desert. The Snake, the Salmon, the upper Hudson—all the other celebrated white torrents—are not in the conversation if the topic is the Colorado. This is still true, although recently (recently in the long span of things, actually within the past forty years) the Colorado has in places been subdued. The country around it is so dry that Dominy's county in Wyoming is a rain forest by comparison. The states of the basin need water, and the Colorado is where the water is. The familiar story of contention for water rights in the Old West—Alan Ladd shooting it out with Jack Palance over some rivulet God knows where—has its mother narrative in the old and continuing story of rights to the waters of the Colorado. The central document is something called the Colorado River Compact, in which the basin is divided in two, at a point close to the Utah-Arizona line. The states of the Upper Basin are allowed to take so much per year. The

Lower Basin gets approximately an equal share. And something gratuitous is passed on to Mexico. The Colorado lights and slakes Los Angeles. It irrigates Arizona. The odd thing about it is that all its writhings and foamings and spectacular rapids lead to nothing. The river rises in the Rockies, thunders through the canyons, and is so used by mankind that when it reaches the Gulf of California, fourteen hundred miles from its source, it literally trickles into the sea. The flow in the big river and in its major tributaries— the Green, the Yampa, the Escalante, the San Juan, the Little Colorado—is almost lyrically erratic, for the volume can vary as much as six hundred per cent from one year to the next. The way to control that, clearly enough, is storage, and this is accomplished under programs developed and administered by the federal Bureau of Reclamation. The Bureau of Reclamation, all but unknown in the American East, is the patron agency of the American West, dispenser of light, life, and water to thirty million people whose gardens would otherwise be dust. Most of the civil servants in the Bureau are Westerners—from the dry uplands as well as the deserts of the Great Basin. They have lived in the problem they are solving, and they have a deep sense of mission. There are many people in the Bureau of Reclamation— perhaps all nine thousand of them—who hope to see the Colorado River become a series of large pools, one stepped above another, from the Mexican border to the Rocky Mountains, with the headwaters of each succeeding lake lapping against the tailrace of a dam. The river and its tributaries have long since been thoroughly surveyed, and

162

throughout the basin damsites of high quality and potentiality stand ready for river diversion, blast excavation, and concrete. Three of these sites are particularly notable here. One is near the juncture of the Green and the Yampa, close to the Utah-Colorado border. The two others are in northern Arizona—in the Grand Canyon. A fourth site would belong in this special list if it were still just a site, but a dam is actually there, in northernmost Arizona, in Glen Canyon. David Brower believes that the dam in Glen Canyon represents the greatest failure of his life. He cannot think of it without melancholy, for he sincerely believes that its very existence is his fault. He feels that if he had been more aware, if he had more adequately prepared himself for his own kind of mission, the dam would not be there. Its gates closed in 1963, and it began backing up water a hundred and eighty-six miles into Utah. The reservoir is called Lake Powell, and it covers country that Brower himself came to know too late. He made his only trips there—float trips on the river with his children—before the gates were closed but after the dam, which had been virtually unopposed, was under construction. Occasionally, in accompaniment to the talks he gives around the country, Brower shows an elegiac film about Glen Canyon, "the place no one knew." That was the trouble, he explains. No one knew what was there. Glen Canyon was one of the two or three remotest places in the United States—far from the nearest road, a hundred and twenty-five miles from the nearest railhead. The film records that the river canyon and its great trellis of side canyons was a deep and sometimes dark world of beauty, where small streams had cut gorges so profound and narrow that people walking in them were in cool twilight at noon, and where clear plunges of water dropped into pools surrounded with maidenhair fern in vaulted grottoes with names like Cathedral in the Desert, Mystery Canyon, Music Temple, Labyrinth Canyon. With all their blue-and-gold walls and darkly streaked water-drip tapestries, these places are now far below the surface of Lake Powell. "Few people knew about these canyons," Brower says quietly. "No one else will ever know what they were like."

The lost worlds of Utah notwithstanding, if conservationists were to label their heroes in the way the English label their generals, David Brower would be known as Brower of the Colorado, Brower of the Grand Canyon. In the early nineteen-fifties, he fought his first major campaign—in his capacity as the first executive director of the Sierra Club—against the dam that the Bureau of Reclamation was about to build near the juncture of the Green and the Yampa. The reservoir would have backed water over large sections of Dinosaur National Monument. In the view of Brower, the Sierra Club, and conservationists generally, the integrity of the National Park system was at stake. The Dinosaur Battle, as it is called, was a milestone in the conservation movement. It was, to begin with, the greatest conservation struggle in half a century—actually, since the controversies that involved the damming of Hetch Hetchy and led to the debates that resulted in the creation, in 1916, of the National Park Service. The Dinosaur Battle is noted as the first time that all the scattered interests of modern conservation—

164

sportsmen, ecologists, wilderness preservers, park advocates, and so forth—were drawn together in a common cause. Brower, more than anyone else, drew them together, fashioning the coalition, assembling witnesses. With a passing wave at the aesthetic argument, he went after the Bureau of Reclamation with facts and figures. He challenged the word of its engineers and geologists that the damsite was a sound one, he suggested that cliffs would dissolve and there would be a tremendous and cataclysmic dam failure there, and he went after the basic mathematics underlying the Bureau's proposals and uncovered embarrassing errors. All this was accompanied by flanking movements of intense publicity— paid advertisements, a film, a book—envisioning a National Monument of great scenic, scientific, and cultural value being covered with water. The Bureau protested that the conservationists were exaggerating—honing and bending the truth—but the Bureau protested without effect. Conservationists say that the Dinosaur victory was the birth of the modern conservation movement—the turning point at which conservation became something more than contour plowing. There is no dam at the confluence of the Green and the Yampa. Had it not been for David Brower, a dam would be there. A man in the public-relations office of the Bureau of Reclamation one day summed up the telling of the story by saying, "Dave won, hands down."

There are no victories in conservation, however. Brower feels that he can win nothing. There is no dam at the Green and the Yampa now, but in 2020 there may be. "The Bureau of Reclamation engineers are like beavers," he says. "They can't stand the sight of running water." Below the Utah-Arizona border, in Marble Gorge, a part of the Grand Canyon, there is likewise no dam. The story is much the same. The Bureau of Reclamation had the dam built on paper, ready to go. A battle followed, and Brower won, hands down. In the Lower Granite Gorge, another part of the Grand Canyon, there is also no dam, and for the same reason. These Grand Canyon battles were the bitterest battles of all. The Bureau felt that Brower capitalized on literary hyperbole and the mystic name of the canyon. He implied, they said, that the dams were going to fill the Grand Canyon like an enormous bathtub, and that the view from the north rim to the south rim would soon consist of a flat expanse of water. Brower's famous advertising campaigns reached their most notable moment at this time. He placed full-page ads in *The New York Times* and the *San Francisco Chronicle*, among other places, under the huge headline "SHOULD WE ALSO FLOOD THE SISTINE CHAPEL SO TOURISTS CAN GET NEARER THE CEILING?" Telegrams flooded Congress, where the battle was decided. The Bureau cried foul, saying that it was intending to inundate only a fraction of one per cent of what Brower was suggesting. The Internal Revenue Service moved in and took away from the Sierra Club the tax-deductibility of funds contributed to it. Contributions to lobbying organizations are not tax-deductible, and the ads were construed as lobbying. The Sierra Club has never recovered its contributions-deductible status, but within the organization it is felt —by Brower's enemies as well as his friends—that the Grand Canyon was worth it. There are no dams in the Grand Can-

166

yon, and in the Bureau of Reclamation it is conceded that there will not be for at least two generations. The defeat of the high dams is frankly credited, within the Bureau, to David Brower. "He licked us." "He had all the emotions on his side." "He did it singlehanded."

Popular assumptions to the contrary, no federal bureau is completely faceless—and, eyeball to eyeball with David Brower, there was a central and predominant figure on the other side of these fights, marshalling his own forces, battling in the rooms of Congress and in the canyon lands of the West for his profound and lifelong belief in the storage of water. This was the Bureau's leader—Floyd E. Dominy, United States Commissioner of Reclamation.

▲

In the District of Columbia, in the labyrinthine fastnesses of the Department of the Interior, somewhere above Sport Fisheries and Wildlife and beyond the Office of Saline Water, there is a complex of corridors lined with murals of enormous dams. This is Reclamation, and these are its monuments: Flaming Gorge Dam, Hungry Horse Dam, Hoover Dam, Glen Canyon Dam, Friant Dam, Shasta Dam, Vallecito Dam, Grand Coulee Dam. I remember the day that I first saw these murals. In the moist and thermoelectric East, they seemed exotic, but hardly more so than the figure to whom the corridors led, the man in the innermost chamber of the maze. The white Stetson was on a table near the door. Behind a magisterial desk sat the Commissioner, smoking a big cigar. "Dominy," he said, shaking hands. "Sit down. I'm a public servant. I don't have any secrets from anybody."

He wore an ordinary Washington suit, but capital pallor was not in his face—a hawk's face, tanned and leathery. He had dark hair and broad shoulders, and he seemed a big man—bigger than his height and weight would indicate—and powerful but not forbidding. "Many people have said of me that I never meet a stranger," he said. "I like people. I like taxi-drivers and pimps. They have their purpose. I like Dave Brower, but I don't think he's the sanctified conservationist that so many people think he is. I think he's a selfish preservationist, for the few. Dave Brower hates my guts. Why? Because I've *got* guts. I've tangled with Dave Brower for many years."

On a shelf behind Dominy's desk, in the sort of central and eye-catching position that might be reserved for a shining trophy, was a scale model of a bulldozer. Facing each other from opposite walls were portraits of Richard M. Nixon and Hoover Dam. Nixon's jowls, in this milieu, seemed even more trapeziform than they usually do. They looked as if they, too, could stop a river. Seeing that my attention had been caught by these pictures, Dominy got up, crossed the room, and stood with reverence and devotion before the picture of Hoover Dam. He said, "When we built that, we—Americans—were the only people who had ever tried to put a high dam in a big river." He said he remembered as if it were his birthday the exact date when he had first seen—as it was then called—Boulder Dam. He had taken a vacation from Campbell County, Wyoming, and driven, with his wife, into the Southwest, and on January 2, 1937, reached the Arizona-Nevada border and got his first view of the dam as he rounded a curve in the road descending toward the gorge of the Colorado. "There she was," he said, looking at the picture in his office. "The first major river plug in the world. Joseph of Egypt learned to store food against famine. So we in the West had learned to store water." He went on to say that he felt sure that—subconsciously, at least—the outline of his career had been formed at that moment. He had begun by building dams seven feet high, and he would one day build dams seven hundred feet high.

The rancher Fred Oedekoven, on whose place Dominy built his first dam, is nearly eighty years old. A tall man, bent slightly forward, he lives in a peeled-log house on the land he homesteaded when he was twenty. I met him once, when I was in the county, and talked with him in the sitting room of his house. Two pictures hung on the walls. One was of Jesus Christ. The other was the familiar calendar scene of the beautiful lake in Jackson Hole, Wyoming, with the Grand Tetons rising in the background. Jackson Lake, as it is called, was built by the Bureau of Reclamation. "When Dominy come here, he took aholt," Oedekoven said. "I hated to see him go. They wanted him to go to Washington, D.C., to go on this water-facilities program, and I advised him to do it, for the advancement. He really clumb up in life."

Dominy had stayed up there as well, becoming the longest-running commissioner in the Department of the Interior. Appointed by Eisenhower, he adapted so well to the indoor range that he was able to keep his position—always "at the pleasure of the President, without term of office"—through two Democratic Administrations, and now he was, in his words, "carrying the Nixon hod." He winked, sat down on the edge of his desk, and pronounced his absorbing code: "Never once have I made a decision against my will if it was mine to make." He had learned to plant creative ideas in senators' and congressmen's minds ("Based on your record, sir, we assume . . ."), when to be a possum, and when to spring like a panther (" 'You get out of my office,' I said. The average bureaucrat would have been shaking, but I wasn't the least bit scared. No member of Congress is going to make me jump through hoops. I've never lost my cool in government work unless I thought it was to my advantage"). He had given crucial testimony against the proposed Rampart Dam, on the Yukon River, arguing that it was too much for Alaska's foreseeable needs; Rampart Dam would have flooded an area the size of Lake Erie, and Dominy's testimony defeated it. He had argued for federal—as opposed to private—power lines leading away from his big dams, thus irritating the special interests of senators and congressmen from several states. "I have been a controversial bastard for many years," he explained, lighting another cigar. Dominy knew his business, though, and he could run a budget of two hundred and forty-five million dollars as if he were driving a fast bus. He had cut down the Bureau's personnel from seventeen thousand to ten thousand. And he

170

had built his stupendous dams. On the wall of his office there was also a picture of Dominy—a bold sketch depicting his head inside a mighty drop of water. It seemed more than coincidence that in an age of acronyms his very initials were FED.

Dominy switched on a projector and screened the rough cut of a movie he had had prepared as an antidote to the Sierra Club's filmed elegy to the inundated canyons under Lake Powell. Dominy's film was called "Lake Powell, Jewel of the Colorado," and over an aerial shot of its blue fjords reaching into the red desert a narrator said, "Through rock and sand, canyon and cliff, through the towering formations of the sun-drenched desert, the waters of the Colorado River pause on their way to the sea." Water skiers cut wakes across the water.

"Too many people think of environment simply as untrammelled nature," Dominy commented. "Preservation groups claim we destroyed this area because we made it accessible to man. Six hundred thousand people a year use that lake now."

The film showed a Navajo on horseback in a blazing-red silk shirt. "Into his land came Lake Powell, which he has woven into his ancient ways," said the narrator.

"Right," said Dominy. "Now people can fish, swim, water-ski, sun-bathe. Can't you imagine going in there with your family for a weekend, getting away from everybody? But Mr. Brower says we destroyed it."

"The canyon lay isolated, remote, and almost unknown to the outside world," said the narrator, "until"—and at that moment a shot of the red walls of Glen Canyon came on the screen, and suddenly there was a great blast and the walls crumbled in nimbuses of dust. Ike had pressed a button. Bulldozers followed, and new roads, and fifty thousand trucks. Cut to dedication of dam, ten years later. "I am proud to dedicate such a significant and beautiful man-made resource," said Lady Bird Johnson. "I am proud that man is here."

Dominy blew smoke into the scene as Lady Bird dissolved. "The need for films of this kind, for public information, is great, because of those who would have all forests and rivers remain pristine," he said. "People ignore facts and play on emotions."

There were more scenes of the blue, still water, lapping at high sandstone cliffs—panoramic vistas of the reservoir. An airplane now appeared over the lake—twin-engine, cargo. "Watch this," Dominy said. "Just watch this." What appeared to be a contrail paid out behind the plane—a long, cloudy sleeve that widened in the air. "Trout!" Dominy said. "Trout! Those are fingerling trout. That's how we put them in the lake."

Montages of shots showed the half-filled lateral canyons —Forgotten Canyon, Cascade Canyon, Reflection Canyon, Mystery Canyon—with people swimming in them, camping beside them, and singing around fires. "In this land, each man must find his own meanings," said the narrator. "Lake Powell, Jewel of the Colorado, offers the opportunity."

"Reclamation is the father of putting water to work for man—irrigation, hydropower, flood control, recreation,"

Dominy said as he turned on the lights. "Let's *use* our environment. Nature changes the environment every day of our lives—why shouldn't *we* change it? We're part of nature. Just to give you a for-instance, we're cloud-seeding the Rockies to increase the snowpack. We've built a tunnel under the Continental Divide to send water toward the Pacific that would have gone to the Atlantic. The challenge to man is to do and save what is good but to permit man to progress in civilization. Hydroelectric power doesn't pollute water and it doesn't pollute air. You don't get any pollution out of my dams. The unregulated Colorado was a son of a bitch. It wasn't any good. It was either in flood or in trickle. In addition to creating economic benefits with our dams, we regulate the river, and we have created the sort of river Dave Brower dreams about. Who are the best conservationists—doers or preservationists? I can't talk to preservationists. I can't talk to Brower, because he's so Goddamned ridiculous. I can't even reason with the man. I once debated with him in Chicago, and he was shaking with fear. Once, after a hearing on the Hill, I accused him of garbling facts, and he said, 'Anything is fair in love and war.' For Christ's sake. After another hearing one time, I told him he didn't know what he was talking about, and said I wished I could show him, I wished he would come with me to the Grand Canyon someday, and he said, 'Well, save some of it, and maybe I will.' I had a steer out on my farm in the Shenandoah reminded me of Dave Brower. Two years running, we couldn't get him into the truck to go to market. He was an independent bastard that nobody could

173

corral. That son of a bitch got into that truck, busted that chute, and away he went. So I just fattened him up and butchered him right there on the farm. I shot him right in the head and butchered him myself. That's the only way I could get rid of the bastard."

"Commissioner," I said, "if Dave Brower gets into a rubber raft going down the Colorado River, will you get in it, too?"

"Hell, yes," he said. "Hell, yes."

▲

Mile 130. The water is smooth here, and will be smooth for three hundred yards, and then we are going through another rapid. The temperature is a little over ninety, and the air is so dry that the rapid will feel good. Dominy and Brower are drinking beer. They have settled into a kind of routine: once a day they tear each other in half and the rest of the time they are pals.

Dominy is wearing a blue yachting cap with gold braid, and above its visor in gold letters are the words "LAKE POWELL." His skin is rouge brown. His nose is peeling. He wears moccasins, and a frayed cotton shirt in dark, indeterminate tartan, and long trousers secured by half a pound of silver buckle. He has with him a couple of small bags and a big leather briefcase on which is painted the great seal of the Bureau of Reclamation—snow-capped mountains, a reservoir, a dam, and irrigated fields, all within the framing shape of a big drop of water. Dominy has been discoursing on the multiple advantages of hydroelectric power, its immediacy ("When you want it, you just throw a switch") and its innocence of pollution.

"Come on now, Dave, be honest," he said. "From a conservationist's point of view, what is the best source of electric power?"

"Flashlight batteries," Brower said.

Brower is also wearing an old tartan shirt, basically orange, and faded. He wears shorts and sneakers. The skin of his legs and face is bright red. Working indoors and all but around the clock, he has been too long away from the sun. He protects his head with a handkerchief knotted at the corners and soaked in the river, but his King Lear billowing white hair is probably protection enough. He travels light. A miniature duffelbag, eight inches in diameter and a foot long—standard gear for the river—contains all that he has with him, most notably his Sierra Club cup, without which he would be incomplete.

Dominy and Brower are both showing off a little. These organized expeditions carry about a dozen people per raft, and by now the others are thoroughly aware of the biases of the conservationist and the Commissioner. The people are mainly from Arizona and Nevada—schoolteachers, a few students, others from the U.S. Public Health Service. On the whole, I would say that Dominy so far has the edge with them. Brower is shy and quiet. Dominy is full of Irish pub chatter and has a grin as wide as the river.

Cans of beer are known as sandwiches in this red, dry, wilderness world. No one questions this, or asks the reason. They just call out "Sandwich, please!" and a can of Coors comes flying through the air. They catch the beer and drink it, and they put the aluminum tongues inside the cans. I threw a tongue in the river and was booed by everyone. No detritus whatever is left in the canyon. Used cans, bottles—all such things—are put in sacks and go with the raft all the way. The beer hangs in the water in a burlap bag from the rear of the raft, with Cokes and Frescas. The bag is hauled onto the raft before a heavy rapid but rides through the lighter ones.

The raft consists of, among other things, two neoprene bananas ten yards long. These pontoons, lashed to a central rubber barge, give the over-all rig both lateral and longitudinal flexibility. The river sometimes leaps straight up through the raft, but that is a mark of stability rather than imminent disaster. The raft is informal and extremely plastic. Its lack of rigidity makes it safe.

This is isolation wilderness: two or three trails in two hundred miles, otherwise no way out but down the river with the raft. Having seen the canyon from this perspective, I would not much want to experience it another way. Once in a rare while, we glimpse the rims. They are a mile above us and, in places, twelve miles apart. All the flat shelves of color beneath them return the eye by steps to the earliest beginnings of the world—from the high white limestones and maroon Hermit Shales of Permian time to the red sandstones that formed when the first reptiles lived and the vermillion cliffs that stood contemporary with the earliest trees. This Redwall Limestone, five hundred feet thick, is so vulnerable to the infiltrations of groundwater that it has been shaped, in the seas of air between the canyon rims, into red towers and red buttes, pillars, caverns, arches, and caves. The groundwater runs for hundreds of miles between the layers of that apparently bone-dry desert rock and bursts out into the canyon in stepped cascades or ribbon falls. We are looking at such a waterfall right now, veiling away from the Redwall, high above us. There is green limestone behind the waterfall, and pink limestone that was pressed into being by the crushing weight of the ocean at the exact time the ocean itself was first giving up life—amphibious life—to dry land. Beneath the pink and green limestones are green-gray shales and dark-brown sandstones—Bright Angel Shale, Tapeats Sandstone—that formed under the fathoms that held the first general abundance of marine life. Tapeats Sea was the sea that compressed the rock that was cut by the river to create the canyon. The Tapeats Sandstone is the earliest rock from the Paleozoic Era, and beneath it the mind is drawn back to the center of things, the center of the canyon, the cutting plane, the Colorado. Flanked by its Bass Limestones, its Hotauta Conglomerates, its Vishnu Schists and Zoroaster Granites, it races in white water through a pre-Cambrian here and now. The river has worked its way down into the stillness of original time.

Brower braces his legs and grips one of the safety ropes that run along the pontoons. He says, "How good it is to hear a living river! You can almost hear it cutting."

Dominy pulls his Lake Powell hat down firmly around his ears. He has heard this sort of thing before. Brower is suggesting that the Colorado is even now making an ever

177

deeper and grander Grand Canyon, and what sacrilege it would be to dam the river and stop that hallowed process. Dominy says, "I think most people agree, Dave, that it wasn't a river of this magnitude that cut the Grand Canyon."

Brower is too interested in the coming rapid to respond. In this corridor of calm, we can hear the rapid ahead. Rapids and waterfalls ordinarily take shape when rivers cut against resistant rock and then come to a kind of rock that gives way more easily. This is not the case in the Grand Canyon, where rapids occur beside the mouths of tributary creeks. Although these little streams may be dry much of the year, they are so steep that when they run they are able to fling considerable debris into the Colorado—sand, gravel, stones, rocks, boulders. The debris forms dams, and water rises upstream. The river is unusually quiet there—a lakelike quiet—and then it flows over the debris, falling suddenly, pounding and crashing through the boulders. These are the rapids of the Grand Canyon, and there are a hundred and sixty-one of them. Some have appeared quite suddenly. In '1966, an extraordinarily heavy rain fell in a small area of the north rim, and a flash flood went down Crystal Creek, dumping hundreds of tons of rock into the river at Mile 99. This instantly created the Crystal Rapids, one of the major drops in the Colorado. In rare instances—such as the rapid we are now approaching—the river has exposed resistant pre-Cambrian rock that contributes something to the precipitousness of the flow of white water. The roar is quite close now. The standing waves look like blocks of cement.

178

Dominy emits a cowboy's yell. My notes go into a rubber bag that is tied with a string. This is the Bedrock Rapid.

We went through it with a slow dive and climb and a lot of splattering water. We undulated. The raft assumed the form of the rapid. We got very wet. And now, five minutes later, we are as dry and warm as if we were wearing fresh clothes straight out of a dryer. And we are drinking sandwiches.

We have a map that is seven inches high and fifty feet long. It is rolled in a scroll and is a meticulously hand-done contemporary and historical portrait of the Colorado River in the Grand Canyon. River miles are measured from the point, just south of the Utah line, where the Paria River flows into the Colorado—the place geologists regard as the beginning of the Grand Canyon. As the map rolls by, it records who died where. "Peter Hansbrough, one of two men drowned, Mile 24, Tanner Wash Rapids, 1889. . . . Bert Loper upset, not seen again, Mile 24, 1949. . . . Scout found and buried in talus, Mile 43, 1951. . . . Roemer drowned in Mile 89, 1948." The first known run of the river was in 1869, and the second shortly thereafter—both the expeditions of Major John Wesley Powell—and even by 1946 only about a hundred people had ever been through the canyon by river. With the introduction of neoprene rafts—surplus from the Second World War—the figure expanded. Five hundred a year were going through by the middle nineteen-sixties, and the number is now in the low thousands.

"As long as people keep on taking out everything that they bring in, they're not going to hurt the Grand Canyon," Brower says. "Rule No. 1 is 'Leave nothing—not even a dam.'"

Dominy does not hear that. He is busy telling a pretty young gym teacher from Phoenix that he played sixty minutes a game as captain of the ice-hockey team at the University of Wyoming. "I liked the speed. I liked the body contact. I developed shots the defense couldn't fathom."

Dominy is in his sixtieth year and is planning an early retirement, but he looks fifty, and it is not at all difficult to imagine him on a solo dash down the ice, slamming the Denver Maroons into pulp against the boards and breaking free to slap the winning shot into the nets. He once did exactly that. He has the guts he says he has, and I think he is proving it now, here on the Colorado. He may be an athlete, but he can't swim. He can't swim one stroke. He couldn't swim across a goldfish pond. And at this moment it is time for us to put things away and pull ourselves together, because although we are scarcely dry from the Bedrock Rapid, the crescendoing noise we hear is Deubendorff, an officially designated "heavy rapid," one of the thirteen roughest in the canyon. Brower goes quiet before a rapid, and he is silent now. He says he is not much of a swimmer, either. We all have life vests on, but they feel as if they would be about as effective against these rapids as they would be against bullets. That is not true, though. Once in a great while, these rafts turn over, and when they do the people all end up bobbing in the calmer water at the foot of the rapid like a hatful of spilled corks. Riding a rigid boat, Seymour Deubendorff was claimed by this rapid on the Galloway-Stone expedition, in 1909. This we learn from our map. Looking ahead, we see two steep grooves, a hundred and fifty yards apart, that have been cut into the south wall of the river gorge. They are called Galloway Canyon and Stone Canyon, and the streams in them are not running now, but each has thrown enough debris into the river to make a major rapid, and together they have produced Deubendorff. Directly in front of us, a mile ahead and high against the sky, is a broad and beautiful Redwall mesa. The river disappears around a corner to the left of it. Meanwhile, the big, uncompromising mesa seems to suggest a full and absolute stop, as if we were about to crash into it in flight, for spread below it in the immediate foreground is a prairie of white water.

There is a sense of acceleration in the last fifty yards. The water is like glass right up to where the tumult begins. Everything is lashed down. People even take hats and handkerchiefs off their heads and tie them to the raft. Everyone has both hands on safety ropes—everyone but Dominy. He giggles. He gives a rodeo yell. With ten smooth yards remaining, he lights a cigar.

There is something quite deceptive in the sense of acceleration that comes just before a rapid. The word "rapid" itself is, in a way, a misnomer. It refers only to the speed of the white water relative to the speed of the smooth water that leads into and away from the rapid. The white water is faster, but it is hardly "rapid." The Colorado, smooth, flows about seven miles per hour, and, white, it goes perhaps fifteen or, at its whitest and wildest, twenty miles per hour—not very rapid by the standards of the twentieth century. Force of suggestion creates a false expectation. The mere appearance of the river going over those boulders—the smoky spray, the scissoring waves—is enough to imply a rush to fatality, and this endorses the word used to describe it. You feel as if you were about to be sucked into some sort of invisible pneumatic tube and shot like a bullet into the dim beyond. But the white water, though faster than the rest of the river, is categorically slow. Running the rapids in the Colorado is a series of brief experiences, because the rapids themselves are short. In them, with the raft folding and bending—sudden hills of water filling the immediate skyline —things happen in slow motion. The projector of your own existence slows way down, and you dive as in a dream, and gradually rise, and fall again. The raft shudders across the ridgelines of water cordilleras to crash softly into the valleys beyond. Space and time in there are something other than they are out here. Tents of water form overhead, to break apart in rags. Elapsed stopwatch time has no meaning at all.

Dominy emerged from Deubendorff the hero of the expedition to date. Deubendorff, with two creeks spitting boulders into it, is a long rapid for a Grand Canyon rapid—about three hundred yards. From top to bottom, through it all, Dominy kept his cigar aglow. This feat was something like, say, a bumblebee's flying through a field of waving wheat at shock level and never once being touched. Dominy's shirt was soaked. His trousers were soaked. But all the way down the rapid the red glow of that cigar picked its way through the flying water from pocket to pocket of air. Actually, he was lucky, and he knew it. "Lucky Dominy," he said when we moved into quiet water. "That's why they call me Lucky Dominy." The whole raftload of people gave him an organized cheer. And he veiled his face in fresh smoke.

We have now moved under and by the big mesa. Brower watched it silently for a long time, and then softly, almost to himself, he quoted Edith Warner:" 'This is a day when life and the world seem to be standing still—only time and the river flowing past the mesas.' "

Wild burros stand on a ledge and look at us from above, right. All burros are on the right, all bighorns on the left. Who knows why? We have entered the beauty of afternoon light. It sharpens the colors and polishes the air.

Brower says, "Notice that light up the line now, Floyd. Look how nice it is on the barrel cactus."

"Gorgeous," says Dominy.

The river is in shadow, and we have stopped for the night where a waterfall arcs out from a sandstone cliff. This is Deer Creek Falls, and it is so high that its shafts of plunging water are wrapped in mist where they strike a deep pool near the edge of the river. The campsite is on the opposite bank. Brower has half filled his Sierra Club cup with water and is using it as a level with which to gauge the height of the falls. His measuring rod is his own height at eye level. Sighting across the cup, he has painstakingly climbed a talus slope behind us, adding numbers as he climbed, and he is now a small figure among the talus boulders at the level of the lip of the waterfall across the river. He calls down that the waterfall is a hundred and sixty feet high. With the raft as a ferry, we crossed the river an hour or so ago and stood in the cool mist where the waterfall whips the air into wind. We went on to climb to the top of the fall and to walk above the stream through the gorge of Deer Creek. The creek had cut a deep, crenellated groove in the sandstone, and for several hundred yards, within this groove, we moved along a serpentine ledge high above the water, which made a great deal of sound below, within the narrow walls of the cut. Brower walked along the ledge—it was sometimes only a foot wide—as if he were hurrying along a sidewalk. At the beginning, the ledge was perhaps fifty feet above the foaming creek, and gradually, up the gorge, the ledge and the creek bed came closer together. Brower just strode along, oblivious of the giddy height. In that strange world between walls of rock, a butterfly flickered by, and he watched it with interest while his feet moved surely forward, never slowing. "Viceroy," he said.

I am afraid of places like that, and my legs were so frozen that I couldn't feel the ledge underfoot. I suggested that we stop and wait for Dominy, who had started later and had said he would catch up. This would obviously provide a good rest, because where Dominy comes from the narrowest ledge is at least three hundred miles wide, and I thought if he was still coming along this one he was probably on his hands and knees. Just then, he came walking around a shoulder of the rock face, balanced above the gorge, whistling. We moved on. Where the ledge met the creek bed, the walls of the gorge widened out and the creek flowed in clear, cascading pools among cactus flowers and mariposa lilies under stands of cottonwood. A scene like that in a context of unending dry red rock is unbelievable, a palpable mirage. Brower walked in the stream and, after a while, stopped to absorb his surroundings. Dominy, some yards behind, had an enamelled cup with him, and he dipped it into the stream. Lifting it to his lips, he said, "Now I'll have a drink of water that has washed Dave Brower's feet."

The water was cold and very clear. Brower scooped some for himself, in his Sierra Club cup. "Any kind of water in country like this is good, but especially when man isn't hogging it for his own use," he said.

Watercress grew around the plunge pools of the short cascades—watercress, growing in cool water, surrounded by thousands of square miles of baking desert rock. Brower took a small bunch in his hand. Bugs were crawling all over it, and he carefully selected leaves and ate them, leaving the bugs behind. "I don't mind sharing my cress with them," he said. "I hope they don't mind sharing it with me."

Brower's snack appealed to Dominy. He waded into the same pool, picked two handfuls of cress, and ate them happily, bugs and all. "Paradise," he said, looking around. "Paradise."

Half obscured in the stream under a bed of cress was the distinctive shimmer of a Budweiser can. Brower picked it up, poured the water out of it, and put it in his pocket.

"When people come in, you can't win," Dominy said, and Brower looked at him with both approval and perplexity.

Inside Dominy's big leather briefcase is a bottle of Jim Beam, and now, at the campsite, in the twilight, with the sun far gone over the rimrocks, we are going to have our quotidian ration—and Dominy is a generous man. After dinner, if patterns hold, he and Brower will square off for battle, but they are at this moment united in anticipation of the bourbon. Big steaks are ready for broiling over the coals of a driftwood fire. There is calm in the canyon. The Commissioner steps to the river's edge and dips a half cup of water, over which he pours his whiskey. "I'm the nation's waterboy," he says. "I need water with my bourbon."

Over the drinks, he tells us that he once taught a German shepherd to climb a ladder. We believe him. He further reminisces about early camping trips with his wife, Alice. They were in their teens when they married. He was state Master Counsellor for the Order of DeMolay, and she was the Queen of Job's Daughters. They had married secretly, and she went with him to the University of Wyoming. "We lived on beans and love," he said. "Our recreation was camping. We went up into the Snowy Range and into the Laramie Peak country, where there was nothing but rattlesnakes, ticks, and us. We used to haul wood down from the mountains to burn for heat in the winter."

Jerry Sanderson, the river guide who has organized this expedition, calls out that dinner is ready. He has cooked an entire sirloin steak for each person. We eat from large plastic trays—the property of Sanderson. Brower regularly ig-

186

nores the stack of trays, and now, when his turn comes, he steps forward to receive his food in his Sierra Club cup. Sanderson, a lean, trim, weathered man, handsome and steady, has seen a lot on this river. And now a man with wild white hair and pink legs is holding out a four-inch cup to receive a three-pound steak. Very well. There is no rapid that can make Sanderson's eyes bat, so why should this? He drapes the steak over the cup. The steak covers the cup like a sun hat. Brower begins to hack at the edges with a knife. Brower in wilderness eats from nothing but his Sierra Club cup.

10 P.M. The moon has moved out in brilliance over the canyon rim. Brower and Dominy are asleep. Dominy snores. Just before he began to snore, he looked at the moon and said, "What's the point of going there? If it were made of gold, we couldn't afford to go get it. Twenty-three billion dollars for landings on the moon. I can't justify or understand that. One, yes. Half a dozen, no. Every time they light a roman candle at Cape Canaveral, they knock four hundred million off other projects, like water storage."

Tonight's fight was about siltation. When Brower finished his steak, he looked across the river at the flying plume of Deer Creek Falls and announced to all in earshot that Commissioner Dominy wished to fill that scene with mud, covering the riverbed and the banks where we sat, and filling the inner gorge of the Colorado right up to within fifty feet of the top of the waterfall.

"That's God-damned nonsense," Dominy said.

Brower explained quietly that rivers carry silt, and that

187

silt has to go somewhere if men build dams. Silt first drops and settles where the river flows into still water at the heads of reservoirs, he said. Gradually, it not only fills the reservoir but also accumulates upstream from the headwaters, and that might one day be the story here at Deer Creek Falls, for Dominy wanted to create a reservoir that would begin only seven miles downstream from our campsite.

"They said Hoover Dam was going to silt up Lake Mead in thirty years," Dominy said. "For thirty years, Lake Mead caught all the God-damned silt in the Colorado River, and Hoover has not been impaired."

"No, but when Mead is low there are forty miles of silt flats at its upper end, and they're getting bigger."

"Not appreciably. Not with Lake Powell three hundred miles upstream."

"Yes, Lake Powell will fill up first."

"When? Tell me *when*?" Dominy was now shouting.

"In a hundred to two hundred years," Brower said quietly.

"That's crap! The figures you work with aren't reliable."

"They come from reliable people."

"Nonsense."

"Oh."

The Colorado, Brower reminded us, used to be known as Old Red. This was because the river was full of red mud. It would never have been possible for Dominy to dip his cup in it in order to get water to go with his bourbon unless he wished to drink mud as well. On arriving at a campsite, rivermen used to fill their boats with water, so that the mud would settle to the bottom of the boats and they would have water for drinking and cooking. Except after flash floods, the Colorado in the Grand Canyon is now green and almost clear, because Lake Powell is catching the silt, and Glen Canyon Dam—fifteen miles upstream from the beginning of the Grand Canyon—is releasing clean water. "Emotionally, people are able to look only two generations back and two generations forward," Brower said. "We need to see farther than that. It is absolutely inevitable, for example, that Lake Powell and Lake Mead will someday be completely filled with silt."

"Nonsense, nonsense, complete nonsense. First of all, we will build silt-detention dams in the tributaries—in the Paria, in the Little Colorado. And, if necessary, we will build more."

"Someday the reservoirs have to fill up, Floyd."

"I wouldn't admit that. I wouldn't admit one inch!"

"Someday."

"*Some*day! Yes, in geologic time, maybe. Lake Powell *will* fill up with silt. I don't know how many thousands of years from now. By then, people will have figured out alternative sources of water and power. That's what I say when you start talking about the geologic ages."

Brower then began to deliver a brief lecture on the phenomenon of aggradation—the term for the final insult that follows when a reservoir is full of silt. Aggradation is what happens to the silt that keeps on coming down the river. The silt piles up and, in a kind of reverse ooze, reaches back upstream many miles, following an inclined plane that rises

189

about eighteen inches per mile—a figure reckoned from the site of the now mud-packed and obsolete dam.

Brower was scarcely halfway through sketching that picture when Dominy ended his contributions with a monosyllabic remark, walked away, put on his pajamas, delivered to the unlistening moon his attack on the space program, and, forgetting Brower and all the silt of years to come, fell asleep. He sleeps on his back, his feet apart, under the mesas.

5 A.M. The sky is light. The air temperature is eighty degrees. Brower sleeps on his side, his knees drawn up.

7 A.M. Eighty-eight degrees. We will soon be on the river. Dominy is brushing his teeth in the green Colorado. Sam Beach, a big, bearded man from White Plains, New York, just walked up to Dominy and said, "I see God has given us good water here this morning."

"Thank you," Dominy said.

And Brower said to Beach, "I imagine that's the first time you ever heard Him speak."

And Beach said, "God giveth, and God taketh away."

▲

What seemed unimaginable beside the river in the canyon was that all that wild water had been processed, like pork slurry in a hot-dog plant, upstream in the lightless penstocks of a big dam. Perspective is where you find it, though, and with this in mind Dominy had taken Brower and me, some days earlier, down into the interior of his indisputable masterpiece, the ten-million-ton plug in Glen Canyon. We had seen it first from the air and then from the rim of Glen Canyon, and the dam had appeared from on high to be frail and surprisingly small, a gracefully curving wafer wedged flippantly into the river gorge, with a boulevard of blue water on one side of it and a trail of green river on the other. No national frontier that I can think of separates two worlds more dissimilar than the reservoir and the river. This frontier has a kind of *douane* as well, administered by men who work in a perfectly circular room deep inside the dam. They wear slim ties and white short-sleeved shirts. They make notes on clipboards. They sit at desks, and all around them, emplaced in the walls of the room, are gauges and dials, and more gauges and dials. To get to this control room, we rode about five hundred feet down into the dam in an elevator, and as we descended Dominy said, "People talk about environment. We're doing something about it." His eyes gleamed with humor. He led us down a long passageway and through a steel door. The men inside stood up. From the devotional look in their eyes, one might have thought that Marc Mitscher had just walked into the engine room of the carrier *Lexington* on the night after the Battle of the Philippine Sea. This was, after all, the man they called the Kmish. Throughout Reclamation, Dominy was known as the Kmish. Standing there, he introduced each man by name. He asked the elevation of Lake Powell.

"Three thousand five hundred and seventy-seven point two zero feet, sir."

Dominy nodded. He was pleased. When the level of the

surface is lowered, a distinct band, known to conservationists as "the bathtub ring," appears along the cliff faces that hold the reservoir. Three thousand five hundred and seventy-seven point two zero would eliminate that, and a good thing, too, for on this day—one hundred years to the sunrise since the day Major Powell reached Glen Canyon on his first expedition—Lake Powell was to be dedicated.

"What are we releasing?" Dominy asked.

"Four thousand three hundred and fifty-six point zero cubic feet per second, sir."

"That's about normal," Dominy said. "Just a little low."

At their consoles, turning knobs, flicking switches, the men in the control room continually create the river below the dam. At that moment, they were releasing something like fourteen hundred tons of water every ten seconds—or, in their terminology, one acre-foot.

"We have eight generating units," Dominy went on. "When we want to make peaking power, we turn them up full and send a wall of water downstream. The rubber rafts operate with licenses, and the guides know the schedule of releases."

Dominy then took us all the way down—down in another elevator, down concrete and spiral stairways, along ever-deeper passageways and down more stairways—until we were under the original bed of the Colorado and at the absolute bottom of the dam, seven hundred and ten feet below the crest. "I don't want Dave Brower to be able to say he didn't see everything," Dominy said—and I could not help admiring him for it, because the milieu he had taken us into could easily be misunderstood. Water was everywhere. Water poured down the spiral staircases. It streamed through the passageways. It fell from the ceilings. It ran from the walls. In some places, sheets of polyethylene had been taped to the concrete. At the bottom, Glen Canyon Dam is three hundred feet thick, but nearly two hundred miles of reservoir was pressing against it, and it had cracked. The Colorado was pouring through. "We may have to get some Dutch boys in here with their thumbs," Dominy said. "The dam is still curing. It hasn't matured yet. So we aren't doing much of anything about this now. We will soon. We have a re-injectionable grouting system; it's an idea I picked up in Switzerland. The crack water is declining anyway. The crack may be sealing itself. It's not serious. You just cannot completely stop the Colorado River."

Brower seemed unable to decide whether he should be shocked by the crack in the dam or impressed by the unvanquishable river. Stalactites had formed on the ceilings of the passageways. I reached up and broke one off. "Don't let Dave Brower see you do that," Dominy said. "You're interrupting nature." Obviously in love with his dam, he scrambled all over it. "When a dam is being built, the concrete is *placed*, not poured," he said, rubbing a hand over a smooth interior wall. "The concrete is barely wet—too dry for pouring. It's put in place with vibrators. We regularly take core samples and send them to Denver for testing—to see if the contractor is meeting specifications. Dave, just to cement our friendship, I'm going to have a pair of bookends made from some of those old core samples for you. Nothing could

193

support a set of Sierra Club books better than a couple of pieces of Glen Canyon Dam. Would you accept that?"

"I'll accept the bookends," Brower said. "Thank you very much, Floyd."

Under the generator room, Dominy led us onto a steel platform inches away from a huge, shining steel generator shaft. The shaft was spinning at who knows how many revolutions per minute, yet the platform around it was scarcely trembling. "Balance," he said proudly. "The secret is balance. In Russia, these platforms vibrate so much they practically knock you down. I know. I've stood on them there." He pointed out sections of giant pipe—penstocks—that contained the Colorado in its passage from reservoir to riverbed. The mighty rapids of the Grand Canyon were now inside that pipe.

Dominy opened a door that led to a strange exterior space—a wide, flat area at the base of the main wall of the dam. Six hundred feet of acutely angled concrete—white and dazzling in the sun—soared up from this level, where Dominy, for purely aesthetic reasons, had somehow imported tons of soil and had planted a smooth and elegant lawn. He called it "the football field," and it was more than large enough to hold one. When visitors peer over the crest of the dam, they look far down its white face to this incongruous lawn, unique in the cosmetics of high dams. From the lawn itself, the thought of the great wall of water on the other side of the dam is unnerving, but no more so than the ten acres of concave concrete up which the eye is led to fragments of red cliff where power-line towers claw at off-plumb angles into a blue swatch of sky. "You don't really appreciate this dam unless you're down on the transformer deck looking up," Dominy said. "Looking down is no way to look at life. You've got to be looking up. Suicides come down that wall sometimes. They don't realize how unvertical it is. When they're found at the bottom, there isn't a God-damned bit of flesh left on them."

Brower said, "My advice to suicides is 'If you've got to go, take Glen Canyon Dam with you.'"

"Read *Desert Solitaire*," Dominy said. "Page 165. The guy who wrote it is way ahead of you."

I eventually bought a copy of *Desert Solitaire*, and found that on page 165 its angry author—Edward Abbey— imagines "the loveliest explosion ever seen by man, reducing the great dam to a heap of rubble in the path of the river. The splendid new rapids thus created we will name Floyd E. Dominy Falls. . . ."

On an overlook not far from the dam, Lake Powell was dedicated by men, white and red, who addressed much of what they said to an unseen enemy, assuming that he was a thousand miles away; he happened to be standing right there. "The Sierra Club to the contrary, I *like* dams," said Governor John Williams of Arizona. When the dam was begun, Williams was a radio announcer, and it was he who broadcast the play-by-play of the original blasting ceremony.

"The Sierra Club notwithstanding, this is a beautiful lake," said Governor Calvin Rampton of Utah, sweeping an arm toward the reservoir. Red cliff walls met the dark-blue water, big buttes stood high in the background, and above it all—immense and alone in the distance—was sacred Navajo Mountain. Far below the overlook, boats wove patterns on the water. Skiers cut crescent wakes. Bunting hung from the speakers' platform in symbolic blue and brown—blue for Lake Powell and brown for the old Colorado.

"A conservationist is one who is content to stand still forever," said Raymond Nakai, of Window Rock, the head of the Navajo Tribal Council. "Major Powell would have approved of this lake. May it ever be brimmin' full." Brower remained silent, but was having difficulty doing so. It was not hard to guess his thoughts. Major Powell—explorer, surveyor, geographer—was not alive to say how he might feel, in English or Navajo.

Then Dominy spoke. "Dave Brower is here today," he said, and the entire ceremony almost fell into the reservoir. "Brower is not here in an official capacity but as my guest," Dominy went on. "We're going to spend several days on Lake Powell, so I can convert him a little. Then we're going down the river, so he can convert me."

▲

Seven years earlier, we could have flown north through Glen Canyon at an altitude of four hundred feet over the riverbed, and that, in a way, is what we did now. We got into a nineteen-foot gray boat—its hull molded for speed, a Buick V-6 engine packed away somewhere, a two-way

196

radio, and the black-lettered words *United States Govern-ment* across the stern—and up the lake we went at twenty knots, for three days spraying arches of clear water toward red-and-black-streaked tapestry walls, pinnacle spires, and monument buttes. The Utah canyonland had been severed halfway up by a blue geometric plane, creating a water-scape of interrupted shapes, spectacularly unnatural, spec-tacularly beautiful. If we stopped for lunch, nudging up to a cool shadowing wall, we were in fact four hundred feet up the sheer side of what had been an immense cliff above the river, and was still an immense cliff—Wingate, Kayenta, Na-vajo Sandstones—above the lake. The boat sped on among hemispherical islands that had once been mountainous domes. It wheeled into Caprian bays. Arched overhangs formed grottoes in what had once been the lofty ceilings of natural amphitheatres.

Above the sound of the engine, Dominy shouted, "Who but Dominy would build a lake in the desert? Look at the country around here! No vegetation. No precipitation. It's just not the setting for a lake under any natural circum-stances. Yet it is the most beautiful lake in the world."

"A thousand people a year times ten thousand years times ten thousand years will never see what was there," Brower said. He pointed straight down into the water. Then he opened a can of beer. The beer was in a big container full of ice. The ice had been made from water of the reservoir—reclaimed pellets of the Colorado. The container held doz-ens of cans of beer and soft drinks, enough for ten men anywhere else, but even on the lake the air was as dry as paper and the sun was a desert sun, and we held those cans in the air like plasma, one after another, all day long. Brower, the aesthetician, likes beer cans. Not for him are the simple biases of his throng. He really appreciates the cans themselves—their cylindrical simplicity, their beautifully crafted lithography. Brower's love of beauty is so powerful it leaps. It sometimes lands in unexpected places. Looking out over the lake at canyon walls flashing in reflected light, he slowly turned his Budweiser in his hand, sipped a little, and then said, "Lake Powell does not exist. I have never seen anything like it before. It's an incredibly beautiful reservoir. It must be the most beautiful reservoir in the world. I just wish you could hold the water level where it is now, Floyd."

Dominy smiled. The lake would become more and more beautiful as it continued to fill, he said. It would go up another hundred and twenty feet, revising vistas as it rose, and the last thirty-five feet would be the most dramatic, because the water at that elevation would reach far into the canyon-land.

"You can't duplicate this experience—this lake—anywhere else," Brower said. "But neither can you enjoy the original experience. That's the trouble. I camped under here once. It was a beautiful campsite. The river was one unending camp-site. The ibis, the egrets, the wild blue herons are gone. Their habitat is gone—the mudbanks along the river."

"We've covered up a lot of nice stuff, there's no question about that, but you've got to admit that as far as views are concerned we've opened up a lot. Look. You can see mountains."

"The Henry Mountains," Brower said. "They were the last mountain range discovered in the lower forty-eight."

For my part, I kept waiting to see the lake. "Lake," as I sensed the word, called to mind a fairly compact water-filled depression in high terrain, with bends and bays perhaps obscuring some parts from others, but with a discernible center, a middle, a place that was farther from shore than any other, and from which a sweeping view of shoreline could be had in all directions. This was a provincialism, based on a Saranac, a Sunapee, a Mooselookmeguntic, and it had left me unprepared for Lake Powell, a map of which looks like a diagram of the human nervous system. The deep spinal channel of Glen Canyon, which was once the path of the Colorado, is now the least interesting part of Lake Powell. The long, narrow bays that reach far into hundreds of tributary canyons are the absorbing places to enter—the boat rounding bends between ever-narrowing walls among reflections of extraordinary beauty on wind-slickened rock. These were the places—these unimaginably deep clefts in the sandstone—that most stirred and most saddened Brower, who remembered wading through clear pools under cottonwood trees four hundred feet below the arbitrary level on which we floated.

In Face Canyon, the boat idled slowly and moved almost silently through still water along bending corridors of rock. "There used to be pools and trees in this little canyon," Brower said. "Cottonwoods, willows."

"Poison ivy, jimsonweed," Dominy said.

"Little parks with grasses. Water always running," Brower went on.

The rock, dark with the oxidation known as desert varnish, appeared to be a rich blue. Desert varnish somehow picks up color from the sky. The notes of a canyon wren descended the pentatonic scale. "That's the music here—the best there is," Brower said. "There used to be paper shells of surface mud on the floor of this canyon, cracking, peeling. Damn it, that was handsome."

"On balance, I can't lament what's been covered up," Dominy said.

In Cascade Canyon, on a ledge that had once been hundreds of feet high, grew a colony of mosses and ferns. "Now there's a hanging garden that's going to get water beyond its wildest dreams," Dominy said. "But unfortunately, like welfare, the water is going to drown it."

In Brower's memory, the most beautiful place in all the region of Glen Canyon was a cavernous space, under vaulting rock walls, that had been named the Cathedral in the Desert. The great walls arched toward one another, forming high and almost symmetrical overlapping parabolas. They enclosed about an acre of ground, in which had grown willows, grasses, columbine, and maidenhair fern. The center of this scene was a slim waterfall, no more than a foot in diameter, that fell sixty feet into a deep and foaming pool. From it a clear stream had flowed through the nave and out to the Colorado. The government boat now entered the Cathedral. Dominy switched off the engine. Water was halfway to the ceiling, and the waterfall was about ten feet high. It was cool in there, and truly beautiful—the vaulted ceiling, the sound of the falling water, the dancing and prismatic reflections, the echo of whispers. It had been beautiful in there before the reservoir came, and it would continue to be so, in successive stages, until water closed the room altogether.

A cabin cruiser came into the Cathedral. In it were a middle-aged couple and an older man. They asked what branch of the government we represented.

"I'm the Commissioner of Reclamation," Dominy said.

"Holy mackerel!" said the younger man.

"This lake is beautiful," the woman said.

"Thank you," Dominy said.

Back in the sunlight, Dominy worried about Brower's lobstering skin. "It would be a terrible thing to get this wildlife enthusiast out here and burn him up," he said.

"I'm red-faced not from the sun but from anger," Brower said.

"Red-faced with anger at my destructive tactics," said Dominy. "See that buoy? That's the Colorado River under water. The buoy is exactly over the original riverbed. Fabulous. Fabulous." The buoy floated on fifty or sixty fathoms of water.

The boat's radio crackled with heavy static as Park Service rangers made contact with one another. One ranger commented on "the unusual companionship" that was loose on the lake.

Dominy gave his cowboy yell, and said, "Hell, if those

rangers could see us now! Dave, in spite of your bad judgment, you're a hell of a nice guy."

"I have nothing but bias," Brower said.

Skiers whipped by, going south. "Some of these bastards come up here and ski for fifty miles," Dominy said.

We cruised into the vicinity of a large natural rock span called Gregory Arch, which was now thirty-five feet beneath us. "If I could swim, I would want to go down and lay a wreath on Gregory Arch, because we've covered it up," Dominy said. "Dave, now that we've cemented our friendship, let me ask you: Why didn't you make a fuss about Gregory Arch?"

"We didn't know about it."

"No one else did, either. No one could have helped you."

"The public's evaluation of a place they may not have ever seen is what will save a place—it is what saved Grand Canyon. It's what might have saved Glen Canyon."

"Saved? For every person who could ever have gotten in here when this place was in its natural state, God damn it, there will be hundreds of thousands who will get in here, into all these side canyons—on the water highways. It's your few against the hundreds. Kids can see this place. Eighty-year-olds. People who can't walk."

"Ninety-nine per cent of the population can walk."

"Before I built this lake, not six hundred people had been in here in recorded history."

"By building this lake," Brower said, "mankind has preëmpted a hundred and eighty-six thousand acres of habitat for its own exclusive use."

"I'm a fair man," said Dominy. "Just to show you how fair

I am, I'll say this: When we destroyed Glen Canyon, we destroyed something really beautiful. But we brought in something else."

"Water."

"You can lament all you want what we covered up. What we got is beautiful, and it's accessible."

The boat, in Labyrinth Canyon, drifted in a film of tamarisk needles, driftwood, bits of Styrofoam, bobbing beer cans, plastic lids. "We conservationists call this Dominy soup," Brower said.

On ledges above the soup were dozens of potholes, some of them very large, and Brower silently drew circles in the air to indicate how, over centuries, these enormous holes in the sandstone had been made by small rocks in swirling water. He and Dominy climbed out of the boat onto a ledge and lowered themselves into a pothole that was eleven feet in diameter and fifteen feet deep. There they began to argue about evaporation—through which, inevitably, a percentage of water in storage will be lost. Six hundred thousand acre-feet of water would annually evaporate from the surface of Lake Powell when full, Brower asserted, and Dominy did not like being baited on his own ground. Something spiralled in his mind like the stones that had cut the hole he was standing in, and eventually he burst out, "Don't give me that evaporation crap! If we didn't store the water, it wouldn't be here."

Brower danced away, came back, and jabbed lightly. "The water is stored only to produce kilowatts anyway," he said.

"We don't release one God-damned acre-foot of water

from Lake Powell just to produce kilowatts," Dominy said.

Brower nodded solemnly in disbelief. He moved in again, shifting his grounds of complaint, and mentioned the huge aeolian sand deposits—millions of tons of fine sand clinging to hollows in the cliffsides—that regularly plop into Lake Powell as the rising water gets to them. Conservationists had suggested that Lake Powell was all but filling with these sands and that the very shores of the lake were crumbling into the water.

"The stuff melts on contact!" Dominy shouted. "You know you're exaggerating! Stretch the truth, that's all you conservationists do. When water hits it, that stuff melts like powder. The unstable material goes, but the walls of Jericho won't come down. The cliffs aren't coming down." He climbed out of the pothole.

Brower pointed to strange striations in jagged shapes on the opposite canyon wall. "That is hieroglyphic, written centuries ago by God Himself," he said.

"Yeah? What does it say?" said Dominy.

"It says, 'Don't flood it.' "

▲

Inevitably, the buoys and the floating directional signs of Lake Powell lead to the Rainbow Bridge Marina, the only source of food or fuel within a radius of fifty miles—a floating hamlet where merchants and Park Service rangers live in structures built on pontoons and drums. No other design solution was possible in a place where the lake surface keeps rising, and sometimes temporarily falling, between shores of sheer stone wall. On the decks of this marina, the people of Lake Powell congregate—campers, skiers, rangers, Reclamation men—and it was here that the sway of Dominy, if it had not been altogether evident before, was displayed in full. From cabin cruiser to cabin cruiser, his name spread everywhere within moments of his arrival, and as he moved along the nonskid marina decks he was regarded as a kind of god, creator of the unending blue waters. A child asked for his autograph. People thanked him repeatedly for the lake. The Kmish winked, and told them they were welcome. He also handed me his camera, put his arm around Brower, and said he wanted a visual record that such a moment had actually happened.

Brower captioned the picture, "Brower gives up."

Moving on from the marina, we tied up the boat at a small wooden dock where the water of Lake Powell met the dry bed of Aztec Creek, and we walked a mile or so uphill among the boulders of the arroyo. Now Brower and Dominy stood under Rainbow Bridge, and there they reopened a running battle they had fought for ten years.

Rainbow Bridge was formed—in an era when the land was uplifting—by waters that raced off Navajo Mountain and punched through a sandstone wall. Pushing gravel and boulders through the opening, cutting down and cutting wide, the creek, in centuries, made the gigantic stone span that crosses it now. Thick and red, immense against the sky, it would fit over the national Capitol dome. It is the largest known natural bridge on earth. When Lake Powell is full, still water will reach into the deep groove of the creek bed below Rainbow Bridge and will fill it to a level twenty-two feet below the base of the span. To Brower, this is simple sacrilege. To Dominy, it is a curious and agreeable coincidence that the water will stop just there.

There have been fly-ins, hike-ins, Congressional hearings. Brower wants a cutoff dam to keep the lake out of the creek bed under the bridge, a diversion dam above the bridge to make the creek—when it runs—run elsewhere, and a diesel pumping station to move the diverted water. Dominy and Brower were standing like two chinch bugs under the enormous stone arch. In a curious reversal of roles, Dominy told Brower that he was "a pyramid builder," that his cutoff dam and diversion dam would cost twenty-five million dollars, and that a little still water beneath the bridge would do far less damage to the natural setting that Brower was trying to preserve than would a pair of flanking dams. Brower said that water under the bridge would undermine its foundations. Dominy said geologists had told him that still water would do far less damage over the years than the flash floods that now go through there. Brower said he did not believe Dominy's geologists. Moreover, he said, Dominy had not taken into account the eventual problem of aggraded silt, which would one day pack the pillars of the bridge in mud.

If there was one concept Dominy had had enough of for a lifetime, it was aggraded silt—all these conservationists telling him about the high-piling ooze that was inescapably going to rise above his clotted reservoirs.

"It won't build back into here, God damn it!" he shouted.

"Yes, it will," Brower said, in a low, firm voice.

"What are you talking about—two hundred years from now?"

"No. About three hundred and fifty. Luna Leopold says that silt aggradation will be eighty feet here."

"That's what he says. I say it's crap. You conservationists say we are destroying Rainbow Bridge simply because we are making it available to people."

The two men walked around for a while, not saying anything, looking up in awe at the bridge. The spanning rock is forty feet thick. It could support a highway. Curiously, it is in more danger from sonic booms than from water. It shakes when booms hit it.

Two hikers appeared from up the creek bed. They had on backpacks, and had come to the bridge overland from Navajo Mountain, an extremely rugged journey. They were college age. One was from Bethesda, the other from St. Louis. We all shook hands, each person giving his name. One of the hikers said, "Did you say 'Dave *Brower*'?"

"Yes," said Brower.

"Dave *Brower*?" the boy repeated. Then, almost to himself, he said it again. "Dave Brower."

I wondered if the hiker was going to bend over and draw a picture of a fish in the sand.

Dominy said, "You're happy to meet *him?* How would you like to meet the Commissioner of Reclamation?"

Perhaps because they were from Missouri and Maryland, neither of the young men had any idea what the term meant, or where the commissioner of whatever it was might be, nor did they ask.

"Dave *Brower*."

They went with us all the way down the trail to the waterhead and the government boat. They stood there, watching Brower, as we pulled away. Without moving, they watched him until we passed out of sight around a bend. Briefly, we came into their view again. They were still watching.

▲

"His supporters believe that the prophet can do no wrong."

"Conservation is a religious movement. So you get sects. And then you have the art of exposition of the individual creed. Each sectarian knows that he is right. Dave Brower has been the prophet leading the faithful."

"The Sierra Club itself is a religious movement."

"If the prophet goes off the straight and narrow course, he becomes more of an adversary than the adversary in the distance."

"He has been bitten by the worm of power."

"He has jumped in front of a moving car, which he was driving."

"Dave *had* to violate orders of the board, in order to get done what he had to do."

"He once said he had thousands of volunteers working with him and that if he ever tried to do things himself there would be one person instead of thousands. And that, tragically, is what has happened in recent years."

"The power structure broke down, or there was insubordination, depending on how you want to look at it."

"He has become, over the years, increasingly less tolerant of the conservation opposition. He used to be far more flexible in his attitude toward the conservation problem."

"This is why the Sierra Club membership has grown, however. He has built it from seven thousand to seventy-seven thousand. People, particularly younger people, flock to the cause. They are fed up with traditional attitudes. Brower once had a willingness to see the other point of view, but now he is a flaming firebrand, and he has split the Sierra Club right down the middle."

"He wasn't arrogant once, but he is now."

"I think that's a fair statement."

"I don't think 'arrogant' is really the right word. You wouldn't associate arrogance with Jesus Christ, for example. I don't mean to make a comparison there."

"With tact, he could have avoided his present trouble. He is stubborn. He's just God-damned stubborn."

"His concern is wilderness. He doesn't really care what happens to people."

"There is a pre-Eden strain in Dave—no question."

"I will say this: I prefer Dave's vices to the virtues of his enemies."

"They are crucifying him, and they are self-congratulating bourgeoisie."

The people who said these things eddied in the Empire Room of the Hotel Sir Francis Drake, in San Francisco,

209

where—four or five hundred in all—they awaited the gavel that would begin the most momentous meeting of the directors of the Sierra Club in the fifty-five years since the defeat of John Muir. There were bearded men in open shirts who appeared to have walked directly in from the trail. There were good-looking women with hairbands, an advertising writer with a Beethoven haircut, at least twenty members of the press, a television-news crew. There were a preponderant number of old people, very local, very San Franciscan people—old bankers in vested suits, with fine memories of Sierra Club high trips in the nineteen-twenties, old men on canes who had reached into low reserves of energy just to be there, because they felt that Brower had expanded their club beyond recognition and had therefore, in a sense, usurped it. They had come in for the kill.

"He is financially reckless."

"He has impugned the motives of the opposition."

"He has disobeyed the directives of the board."

"There has been a growth in ecological sophistication in the United States over the past twenty years, and Dave has in part caused it."

"He is a high-risk politician, that's all. He risked his neck and he lost."

"He has a death wish."

"He's been edging toward it all the time."

"He loved his job, and was always pushing things to the point where he might lose it."

"He is a great practitioner of brinkmanship, and this time he went much too far."

"He is a shy man who thrusts himself forward—onstage. He is a freewheeling, farseeing visionary when he is not trapped, and he is a rigid personality when he is trapped."

"Sometimes he seems paranoid. He believes that the Park Service, the Forest Service, the Pacific Gas and Electric Company are out to get him. We always told him, 'No one outside the Sierra Club is going to get you. The only person who'll get you is you.'"

"What will he do? Do you think he would ever go into private industry?"

"He would open his own waffle shop first."

There was a U-shaped table at one end of the room, faced by hundreds of funeral chairs. People read the *Chronicle* while they waited. A celebrated tree in the Sierra Nevada— a giant sequoia with a roadway running through it—had crashed to the ground. The paper reprinted on the front page Ansel Adams' famous old photograph of the tree—the Wawona Tunnel Tree, as it was called—with a Pierce-Arrow nosing into it and a couple of figures standing beside the Pierce-Arrow. No one seemed to be getting much past the front page. Although the outcome of the meeting was a fore-gone conclusion, the atmosphere was tense. David Brower was going to be ejected as executive director of the Sierra Club. A last-minute resignation notwithstanding, "ejected" was the word. The executive director was an employee of the board of directors, and the board of directors was going to throw him out. The actual showdown had come in a mail-ballot election of new members of the board. Brower himself and a slate of his allies had been candidates, and they had lost, hands down. Supporters of Brower remained on the board, but the balance of power was now against him. Right to the end, Brower held on to the hope that somehow a majority of the fifteen directors would—all their expressed attitudes and commitments to the contrary— decide to keep him on, but he was the only person in the Sir Francis Drake Hotel who was that naïve. Whatever the terms might be, today's event would be a rite of expurgation.

"As his success grew, he paid less and less attention to what people in the club were thinking and saying. I don't think the man changed so much as he developed. He began to think, I *am* the Sierra Club."

"He is a combination poet, naturalist, and politician, a generalist in the fight to save the environment. He is tough enough to get into the thick of back-alley fights. He thinks that to win fights you have to have uncompromising militancy. The tax-exemption thing illustrates the risks he has been willing to take."

"No one in the Sierra Club faults him for that."

"I think Dave is right in feeling that militancy is the stance the Sierra Club should take if it is to be true to the spirit of John Muir."

"He started on five-sevenths pay and he worked seven-fifths of the time. His trouble was that he could not take direction. He was unapproachable. He tried to claim all the rights of an individual while representing an organization."

"He was the most effective single force in the conservation effort in this country. And he still is."

The gavel rapped. The room fell silent. Seated at the U-shaped table was the high tribunal of the Sierra Club.

Martin Litton, writer. Portola Valley, California. Big, outspoken man, bitter for the cause. Courageous. He goes down the Colorado in rigid boats. Pro-Brower.

Patrick D. Goldsworthy, biochemist. University of Washington. Wilderness mountain man but not a rope-and-piton climber. Defender of the North Cascades. Pro-Brower.

Eliot Porter, one of the two great wilderness photographers in the world. Tusuque, New Mexico. Medical doctor. Never practiced. Pro-Brower.

Larry Moss, nuclear engineer. Tanzania, California. White House Fellow. No outdoor specialty. Pro-Brower.

Raymond Sherwin, Superior Court judge. Vallejo, California. No outdoor specialty. Anti-Brower.

August Frugé, director of the University of California Press, Berkeley. Brower's boss when Brower worked there. No outdoor specialty. Anti-Brower.

Will Siri, biophysicist. University of California, Berkeley. Mountaineer. Co-leader in 1954 of the Makalu expeditions in the Himalayas. Cordillera Blanca, Peru, 1952. Everest, 1963. Anti-Brower.

"Say what you will about financial irresponsibility or in-subordination, what's really going on here is a deep death struggle between mountaineers. Siri and others. Mountain-eers are individualists—loners. Brower is an individualist, a loner."

"Brower is a mountaineer."

"Not a single climber he grew up with is still a friend of his."

"They've all turned on him."

"There is no love-hate like the love-hate that exists among mountaineers."

Philip Berry, lawyer, climber, mountaineer. Age, thirty-one. Grew up in Berkeley. Frequent visitor, throughout his youth, in Brower's home. Brower taught him climbing tech-niques. Brower and Berry once attempted a new route up Mount Clarence King, in the Sierra. Brower loosened a rock that hit Berry. Duck hunter. Anti-Brower.

Richard Leonard. Former president of the Sierra Club. Four years older than Brower and long his closest friend. Neighbor of Brower in Berkeley, and in the Mills Tower of-fice building, San Francisco. Original proposer of Brower for membership in the Sierra Club. Nominator of Brower as executive director. Anti-Brower. Said to be the master-mind of the anti-Brower forces. Lawyer, climber, moun-taineer.

From the bottom of the U, Leonard looked out into the room without expression. He appeared to be a man who had never lost, or even mislaid, his composure. Leonard did not so much as turn his head when Martin Litton grabbed a mi-crophone and shouted, "This election has been rife with per-jury, calumny, and fraud!" Leonard, short and unprepossess-ing, cleared his throat at regular intervals. Nothing of his climbing past showed in his legal present. He and Brower—tied together—had climbed more mountains than either could remember. Among the people Leonard could see from his seat at the U-shaped table was Brower, standing at the edge of the crowd, his chin up, his white hair focal in the room. What Leonard was thinking then is anyone's guess, but it may have been something close to a commentary he had made in private only hours before.

"In the early years, Dave was absolutely magnificent as the leader of the club. He fought vigorously, aggressively, and—the point I want to emphasize—courteously. In later years, he started into his philosophy that Nice Nelly could never do the job. He impugned the motives of Forest Ser-vice people, Park Service people, congressmen. He seemed to feel that the end justified the means. The board passed reso-lutions insisting that he wage campaigns on demonstrable facts. Repeatedly, he has disregarded what the board has told him to do. He seems to think that it is he who knows what is best for the Sierra Club and for conservation in the long run, and that the board of directors is just standing in his way. The basis of his drive is that the earth is going to hell fast and something has to be done about it. Because of this, Dave will spend the resources of any organization he is with in unlimited fashion. 'We're not trying to save money, we're trying to save the world,' he will say, and then he will put thirty thousand dollars or so into another newspaper advertisement, without being authorized to do so by the board. I want you to know this, though: He has never taken one dime for himself. One look at his house shows that— how shabby it is, aluminum pans catching the rain. His ideals are good, but his naïveté would eventually destroy the organization. He believes that if he bankrupts the Sierra Club it is in a glorious cause. He was, incidentally, an excellent climber. We began to climb together when he was twenty-one and I was twenty-five. My life depended on his judgment and ability for weeks at a time. We once spent three weeks together on a glacier in British Columbia, sleeping on ice two thousand feet deep. Dave went snow-blind. He thought it was a weakness to use dark glasses. He was convinced that he could adjust his eyes to the sun. The sun's rays will congeal albumin, like cooking an egg. Dave's eyes were closed for two or three days. I think he feels the need to decide medical and optical questions for himself. He also believes, as you know, in self-fulfilling prophecies. The snowball theory of action. Things will work out. Providence has always looked after the Sierra Club and always will,

Dave thinks. I have no personal animosity toward Dave. We just have to save the Sierra Club, that's all."

Richard Sill, physicist. University of Nevada. No outdoor specialty. Anti-Brower.

Paul Brooks, writer on conservation subjects. Lincoln, Massachusetts. Retired executive editor of Houghton Mifflin. Canoeman. Refers to his wife as "the bow paddle." At home, she puts up the storm windows. Anti-Brower.

Edgar Wayburn, San Francisco physician, who grew up in Macon, Georgia. President of the Sierra Club, and long its principal voice of conciliating reason. Describes Brower as "a creative genius." Anti-Brower.

Maynard Munger, realtor. Lafayette, California. No outdoor specialty. Campaigned for the board of directors with a photograph of himself in a kayak. Feels that the Sierra Club enhances his image as a realtor. Anti-Brower.

Ansel Adams, the other great wilderness photographer in the world. Carmel, California. Met Brower on a knapsack trip in the High Sierra in 1933. Strong personal and professional relationship with Brower over the years. Anti-Brower.

Adams, a burly, black-bearded man, knew a detail of which only one other person in the room was in all likelihood aware. Under the big tree, beside the Pierce-Arrow, in the Ansel Adams photograph that was on the front page of that day's *Chronicle* stood David Brower—indistinguishable,

217

unidentified, but present, in a picture that was captioned "A Fallen Giant."

Luna Leopold, hydrologist. Washington, D.C. Sharp mind, sharp tongue. Expert on the Colorado. Expert on river sedimentation. Snowshoe hunter. Son of Aldo Leopold, who wrote *A Sand County Almanac* and *Round River,* literary touchstones of modern conservation-ecology. Pro-Brower.

The event of the day occurred in less time than it would take to tack a notice to a wall. President Wayburn recognized Siri, and Siri said that David Brower was "the greatest spiritual conservation leader of this century." He added, "However, two giants are in conflict—the body of the Sierra Club and the embodiment of David Brower. I move that his resignation be accepted."

Richard Leonard seconded the motion and was hissed as he did so.

Perhaps incredibly, Brower, standing in the back of the room, still felt hopeful. There could be a change of heart.

All in favor? Ten. Opposed? Five. Carried.

In a soft, emotional voice, Brower read a farewell speech that contained no pumice. From its tone, he might have been reading a story to children around a campfire. Then he left the room.

"Expansion cracking" was his term for what had happened. A small, local organization had grown into a major national and international force in the conservation movement, and at each stage there had been people who had wanted to stop. Brower had come to see conservation as inescapably a global and supranational matter, with pollution control and population control its first concerns, *sine qua non* to the preservation of wilderness. The best of his opposition, not necessarily disagreeing, felt that the Sierra Club should have more limited objectives if it was to reach any objectives at all, but Brower, meanwhile, was reaching into the endangered stratosphere and beyond it for the sun and the stars. The money would come from somewhere. It always had.

In the months that followed the meeting at the Sir Francis Drake, Brower went off whenever he could into wilderness areas where, in his words, he put himself back in touch with his purposes. On one of these trips, an aimless wandering through the Sierra Nevada, he found himself drawn, perhaps not so aimlessly, to the grove in the southern Yosemite where the giant sequoia had fallen.

The crash had been sudden and cataclysmic, the impact so great that the enormous tree had broken into pieces as if it were made of crockery. In several places, at intervals of about fifty feet, the trunk had broken clean through. The wood inside looked like red brick. Upper limbs had been driven deep into the ground. Sequoia cones were everywhere, and Brower picked some up. "I am forced to say it was a rough winter on both of us," Brower said to the tree. He climbed the side of the fallen trunk and stood on it, three stories off the ground. He shook a seed out of one of the cones. The cone was no larger than a walnut, and the tiny seed, encased in a winglike fibre, was nothing but a sliver, three-sixteenths of an inch long. "This seed can grow fifty thousand cubic feet of wood that can live for thirty-five hundred years," Brower said, speaking down from the trunk. "This seed knows how to shape an arrowhead canopy, how to design a root system to combat siltation, how to pump water three hundred feet up. This seed has worked for ninety million years and has not been to forestry school." He looked around to see, if he could, why the big tree had fallen. The tunnel in its base had been cut through a burn scar in 1881, and was wide enough for horse-drawn carriages and, until the middle of the twentieth century, for automobiles. But automobiles in recent years had grown too wide, so another roadway had been paved around the tree for cars that could not go through it, and this additional roadway was on the side away from the fall—on the side where the roots had broken. "Too much encroachment on the vitality of a living thing," Brower concluded. "It must have been a hell of a noise, a gorgeous crash. Detroit wins again."

▲

Mile 141. We are in a long, placid reach of the river. The Upset Rapid is eight miles downstream, but its name, all morning, has been a refrain on the raft. People say it as if they were being wheeled toward it on a hospital cart. We have other rapids to go through first—the Kanab Rapid, the Matkatamiba Rapid—but everyone has been thinking beyond them to Upset.

"According to the *River Guide*, there hasn't been a death in the Upset Rapid for a little over two years," someone joked.

"The map says Upset is very bad when the water is low."

"How is the water, Jerry?"

"Low."

"Under today's controlled river, we're riding at the moment on last Sunday's releases," Dominy explained. "This is as low as the river will get under controlled conditions. Tomorrow, Monday's conditions will catch up with us, so things will improve."

"Thank you very much, Commissioner, but what good will Monday's releases do us today?"

"Let's camp here," someone put in.

"It's ten-thirty in the morning."

"I don't care."

"The river has its hands tied, but it's still running," said Brower. "If the Commissioner gets very wet today, it's his own fault."

Jerry Sanderson has cut the engine—a small, cocky outboard that gives the raft a little more speed than the river and is supposed to add some control in rapids. We drift silently.

Brower notices a driftwood log, bleached and dry, on a ledge forty feet above us. "See where the river was before you turned it off, Floyd?"

"I didn't turn it off, God damn it, I turned it on. Ten months of the year, there wasn't enough water in here to boil an egg. My dam put this river in business."

Dominy begins to talk dams. To him, the world is a tessellation of watersheds. When he looks at a globe, he does not see nations so much as he sees rivers, and his imagination runs down the rivers building dams. Of all the rivers in the world, the one that makes him salivate most is the Mekong. There are chances in the Mekong for freshwater Mediterraneans—huge bowls of topography that are pinched off by gunsight passages just crying to be plugged. "Fantastic. Fantastic river," he says, and he contrasts it with the Murrumbidgee River, in New South Wales, where the Australians have spent twenty-two years developing something called the Snowy Mountains Hydroelectric Scheme— "a whole lot of effort for a cup of water." Brower reminds Dominy that dams can break, and mentions the disaster that occurred in Italy in 1963. "That dam didn't break," Dominy tells him. "That dam did *not* break. It was nine hundred feet high. Above it was a granite mountain with crud on top. The crud fell into the reservoir, and water splashed *four hundred feet* over the top of the dam and rushed down the river and killed two thousand people. The dam is still there. It held. Four hundred feet of water over it and it held. Of course, it's useless now. The reservoir is full of crud."

"Just as all your reservoirs will be. Just as Lake Powell will be full of silt."

"Oh, for Christ's sake, Dave, be rational."

"Oh, for Christ's sake, Floyd, *you* be rational."

"Have you ever been *for* a dam, Dave? Once? Ever?"

"Yes. I testified in favor of Knowles Dam, on the Clark Fork River, in Montana. I saw it as a way to save Glacier National Park from an even greater threat. Tell me this, Floyd. Have you ever built a dam that didn't work?"

"Yes, if you want to know the truth. I'm not afraid to tell you the truth, Dave. On Owl Creek, near Thermopolis, Wyoming. Geologic tests were done at one point in the creek and they were O.K., and then the dam was built some distance upstream. We learned a lesson. Never build a dam except exactly where tests are conducted. Cavities developed under the dam, also under the reservoir. Every time we plug one hole, two more show up. Plugs keep coming out. The reservoir just won't fill. Someday I'll tell you another story, Dave. I'll tell you about the day one of our men opened the wrong valve and flooded the *inside* of Grand Coulee Dam."

"I've heard enough."

Dominy and Brower call for sandwiches, open them, and dutifully drop the tongues inside. Brower now attacks Dominy because a dam project near Ventura, California, is threatening the existence of thirty-nine of the forty-five remaining condors in North America. "We've got to get upset about the condor," Brower tells him. "No one likes to see something get extinct."

"The condor was alive in the days of the mastodons," Dominy says. "He is left over from prehistoric times. He can't fly without dropping off something first. He is so huge a kid with a BB gun can hit him. He's in trouble, dam or no dam. If you give him forty thousand acres, he's still in trouble. He *is* in trouble. His chances of survival are slim. I think it would be nice if he survived, but I don't think this God-damned project would have any real bearing on it."

Dominy draws deeply on his beer. He takes off his Lake Powell hat, smooths his hair back, and replaces the hat. I wonder if he is thinking of the scale-model bulldozer in his office in Washington. The bulldozer happens to have a condor in it—a rubber scale-model condor, sitting in the operator's seat.

Dominy's thoughts have been elsewhere, though. "Who was that old man who tried to read poetry at Kennedy's Inaugural? With the white hair blowing all over the place."

"Robert Frost."

"Right. He and I went to Russia together. I was going to visit Russian dams, and he was on some cultural exchange, and we sat beside each other on the plane all the way to Moscow. He talked and talked, and I smoked cigars. He said eventually, 'So you're the dam man. You're the creator of the great concrete monoliths—turbines, generators, stored water.' And then he started to talk poetically about me, right there in the plane. He said, 'Turning, turning, turning . . . creating, creating . . . creating energy for the people . . . for the people. . . .'

"Most of the day, Frost reminisced about his childhood, and he asked about mine, and I told him I'd been born in a town so small that the entrance and exit signs were on the same post. Land as dry and rough as a cob. You'll never see any land better than that for irrigating. God damn, she lays pretty. And he asked about my own family, and I told him about our farm in Virginia, and how my son and I put up nine hundred and sixty feet of fence in one day. I told my son, 'I'll teach you how to work. You teach yourself how to play.'"

We have been through the Kanab Rapid—standing waves six feet high, lots of splash—and we are still wet. It is cold in the canyon. A cloud—a phenomenon in this sky—covers the sun. We are shivering. The temperature plunges if the sun is obscured. The oven is off. Clothes do not quickly dry. Fortunately, the cloud seems to be alone up there.

Mile 144.8. "Here we are," Brower says. He has the map in his hand. Nothing in the Muav Limestone walls around us suggests that we are anywhere in particular, except in the middle of the Grand Canyon. "We are entering the reservoir," Brower announces. "We are now floating on Lake Dominy."

"Jesus," mutters Dominy.

"What reservoir?" someone asks. Brower explains. A dam that Dominy would like to build, ninety-three miles downstream, would back still water to this exact point in the river.

"Is that right, Commissioner?"

"That's right."

The cloud has left the sun, and almost at once we feel warm again. The other passengers are silent, absorbed by what Brower has told them.

"Do you mean the reservoir would cover the Upset

Rapid? Havasu Creek? Lava Falls? All the places we are coming to?" one man asks Dominy.

Dominy reaches for the visor of his Lake Powell hat and pulls it down more firmly on his head. "Yes," he says.

"I'd have to think about that."

"So would I."

"I would, too."

Our fellow-passengers have become a somewhat bewildered—perhaps a somewhat divided—chorus. Dominy assures them that the lake would be beautiful, like Powell, and, moreover, that the Hualapai Indians, whose reservation is beside the damsite, would have a million-dollar windfall, comparable to the good deal that has come to the Navajos of Glen Canyon. The new dam would be called Hualapai Dam, and the reservoir—Brower's humor notwithstanding—would be called Hualapai Lake.

"I'm prepared to say, here and now, that we should touch nothing more in the lower forty-eight," Brower comments. "Whether it's an island, a river, a mountain wilderness—nothing more. What has been left alone until now should be left alone permanently. It's an extreme statement, but it should be said."

"That, my friend, is debatable."

The others look from Brower to Dominy without apparent decision. For the most part, their reactions do not seem to be automatic, either way. This might seem surprising among people who would be attracted, in the first place, to going down this river on a raft, but nearly all of them live in communities whose power and water come from the Colorado. They are, like everyone, caught in the middle, and so they say they'll have to think about it. At home, in New Jersey, I go to my children's schoolrooms and ask, for example, a group of fourth graders to consider a large color photograph of a pristine beach in Georgia. "Do you think there should be houses by this beach, or that it should be left as it is?" Hands go up, waving madly. "Houses," some of the schoolchildren say. Others vote against the houses. The breakdown is fifty-fifty. "How about this? Here is a picture of a glorious mountain in a deep wilderness in the State of Washington. There is copper under the mountain." I list the uses of copper. The vote is close. A black child, who was for houses on the beach, says, "Take the copper." I hold up the Sierra Club's Exhibit-Format book *Time and the River Flowing* and show them pictures of the Colorado River in the Grand Canyon. Someone wants to build a dam in this river. A dam gives electricity and water—light and food. The vote is roughly fifty-fifty.

After Brower ran his ad about the flooding of the Sistine Chapel, Dominy counterattacked by flying down the Colorado in a helicopter, hanging by a strap from an open door with a camera in his hand. He had the pilot set the helicopter down on a sandbar at Mile 144.8, and he took a picture straight down the river. The elevation of the sandbar was eighteen hundred and seventy-five feet above sea level. Taking pictures all the way, Dominy had the pilot fly at that exact altitude down the river from the sandbar to the site of

227

Hualapai Dam. ("That pilot had the God-damned props churning right around the edge of that inner-gorge wall, and he was *noivous,* but I made him stay there.") At the damsite, the helicopter was six hundred feet in the air. Dominy took his collection of pictures to Congress. "Brower says we want to ruin the canyon. Let's see whether we're going to ruin it," he said, and he demonstrated that Hualapai Lake, for all its length, would be a slender puddle hidden away in a segment of the Grand Canyon that was seven miles wide and four thousand feet deep. No part of the lake would be visible from any public observation point in Grand Canyon National Park, he told the congressmen. "Hell, I know more about this river than the Park Service, the Sierra Club, and everyone else," he says, finishing the story. "I took my pictures to Congress because I thought that this would put the ball in their court, and if they wanted to field it, all right, and if they wanted to drop it, that was all right, too."

We have gone through Matkatamiba and around a bend. Jerry Sanderson has cut the motor again, and we are resting in the long corridor of flat water that ends in the Upset Rapid. There is a lot of talk about "the last mile," the low water, "the end of the rainbow," and so on, but this is just fear chatter, dramatization of the unseen.

"Oh, come on, now. One of these rafts could go over Niagara Falls."

"Yes. With no survivors."

Brower hands Dominy a beer. "Here's your last beer," he

says. It is 11 A.M., and cool in the canyon. Another cloud is over the sun, and the temperature is seventy-seven degrees. The cloud will be gone in moments, and the temperature will go back into the nineties.

"Here's to Upset," Brower says, lifting his beer. "May the best man win."

The dropoff is so precipitous where Upset begins that all we can see of it, from two hundred yards upstream, is what appears to be an agglomeration of snapping jaws—the leaping peaks of white water. Jerry cannot get the motor started. "It won't run on this gas," he explains. "I've tried river water, and it won't run on that, either." As we drift downstream, he works on the motor. A hundred and fifty yards. He pulls the cord. No sound. There is no sound in the raft, either, except for the *psss* of a can being opened. Dominy is having one more beer. A hundred yards. Jerry starts the motor. He directs the raft to shore. Upset, by rule, must be inspected before the running.

We all got off the raft and walked to the edge of the rapid with Sanderson. What we saw there tended to erase the thought that men in shirtsleeves were controlling the Colorado inside a dam that was a hundred and sixty-five river miles away. They were there, and this rapid was here, thundering. The problem was elemental. On the near right was an enormous hole, fifteen feet deep and many yards wide, into which poured a scaled-down Canadian Niagara

—tons upon tons of water per second. On the far left, just beyond the hole, a very large boulder was fixed in the white torrent. High water would clearly fill up the hole and reduce the boulder, but that was not the situation today.

"What are you going to do about this one, Jerry?"

Sanderson spoke slowly and in a voice louder than usual, trying to pitch his words above the roar of the water. "You have to try to take ten per cent of the hole. If you take any more of the hole, you go in it, and if you take any less you hit the rock."

"What's at the bottom of the hole, Jerry?"

"A rubber raft," someone said.

Sanderson smiled.

"What happened two years ago, Jerry?"

"Well, the man went through in a neoprene pontoon boat, and it was cut in half by the rock. His life jacket got tangled in a boat line, and he drowned."

"What can happen to the raft, Jerry?"

"Oh, parts of them sometimes get knocked flat. Then we have to stop below the rapid and sew them up. We have a pump to reinflate them. We use Dacron thread, and sew them with a leather punch and a three-inch curved needle. We also use contact adhesive cement."

"Wallace Stegner thinks this river is dead, because of Glen Canyon Dam, but I disagree," Brower said. "Just look at it. You've got to have a river alive. You've just got to. There's no alternative."

"I prefer to run this rapid with more water," Sanderson said, as if for the first time.

230

"If you want to sit here twenty-four hours, I'll get you whatever you need," said Dominy.

Sanderson said, "Let's go."

We got back on the raft and moved out into the river. The raft turned slightly and began to move toward the rapid. "Hey," Dominy said. "Where's Dave? Hey! We left behind one of our party. We're separated now. Isn't he going to ride?" Brower had stayed on shore. We were now forty feet out. "Well, I swear, I swear, I swear," Dominy continued, slowly. "He isn't coming with us." The Upset Rapid drew us in.

With a deep shudder, we dropped into a percentage of the hole—God only knows if it was ten—and the raft folded almost in two. The bow and the stern became the high points of a deep V. Water smashed down on us. And down it smashed again, all in that other world of slow and disparate motion. It was not speed but weight that we were experiencing: the great, almost imponderable, weight of water, enough to crush a thousand people, but not hurting us at all because we were part of it—part of the weight, the raft, the river. Then, surfacing over the far edge of the hole, we bobbed past the incisor rock and through the foaming outwash.

"The great outdoorsman!" Dominy said, in a low voice. "The great outdoorsman!" He shook water out of his Lake Powell hat. "The great outdoorsman standing safely on dry land wearing a God-damned life jacket!"

The raft, in quiet water, now moved close to shore, where Brower, who had walked around the rapid, stood waiting.

231

"For heaven's sake, say nothing to him, Floyd."

"Christ, I wouldn't think of it. I wouldn't dream of it. What did he do during the war?"

The raft nudged the riverbank. Dominy said, "Dave, why didn't you ride through the rapid?"

Brower said, "Because I'm chicken."

▲

A Climber's Guide to the High Sierra (Sierra Club, 1954) lists thirty-three peaks in the Sierra Nevada that were first ascended by David Brower. "*Arrowhead.* First ascent September 5, 1937, by David R. Brower and Richard M. Leonard. . . . *Glacier Point.* First ascent May 28, 1939, by Raffi Bedayan, David R. Brower, and Richard M. Leonard. . . . *Lost Brother.* First ascent July 27, 1941, by David R. Brower. . . ." Brower has climbed all the Sierra peaks that are higher than fourteen thousand feet. He once started out at midnight, scaled the summit of Mount Tyndall (14,025) by 3 A.M., reached the summit of Mount Williamson (14,384) by 7 A.M., and was on top of Mount Barnard (14,003) at noon. He ate his lunch—nuts, raisins, dried apricots—and he went to sleep. He often went to sleep on the high peaks. Or he hunted around for ice, removing it in wedges from cracks in the granite, sucking it to slake his thirst. If it was a nice day, he would stay put for as much as an hour and a half. "The summit is the anticlimax," he says. "The way up is the thing. There is a moment when you know you have the mountain by the tail. You figure out how the various elements go together. You thread the route in your mind's eye, after hunting and selecting, and hitting dead ends. Finally, God is good enough. He built the mountain right, after all. A pleasant surprise. If you don't make it and have to go back, you play it over and over again in your mind. Maybe this would work, or that. Several months, a year, or two years later, you do it again." When Brower first tried to climb the Vazquez Monolith, in Pinnacles National Monument, he was stopped cold, as had been every other climber ever, for the face of the monolith was so smooth that Brower couldn't even get off the ground. Eventually, someone else figured out how to do that, but, as it happened, was stopped far shy of the summit. When Brower heard about this, he went to his typewriter, wrote a note identifying himself as the first man to ascend Vazquez Monolith, and slipped the note into a small brass tube. In his mind, he could see his route as if he were carrying a map. He went to Pinnacles National Monument, went up the Vazquez Monolith without an indecisive moment, and, on top, built a cairn around the brass tube. When Brower led a group to Shiprock in 1939, at least ten previous climbing parties had tried and failed there. Shiprock is a seven-thousand-foot monadnock that looks something like a schooner rising in isolation from the floor of the New Mexican desert. Brower studied photographs of Shiprock for many months, then planned an ornately complicated route—about three-quarters of the way up one side, then far down another side, then up a third and, he hoped, final side, to the top. That is how the climb went, without flaw, start to finish. Another brass tube. "I like mountains. I like granite. I particularly like the feel of the Sierra granite. When I climbed the Chamonix Aiguilles, the granite felt so much like the granite in the Yosemite that I felt right at home. Once, in the Sierra, when I was learning, I was going up the wall of a couloir and I put both hands and one knee on a rock. The rock moved, and fell. It crashed seventy-five feet below. One of my hands had shot upward, and with two fingers I caught a ledge. I pulled myself up, and I sat there on that ledge and thought for a long while. Why was I that stupid—to put that much faith in one rock? I have an urge to get up on top. I like to get up there and see around. A three-hundred-and-sixty-degree view is a nice thing to have. I like to recognize where I've been, and look for routes where I might go."

▲

Mile 156. Already the talk is of Lava Falls, which lies twenty-four miles ahead but has acquired fresh prominence in the aftermath of Upset. On the table of rated rapids—copies of which nearly everyone is at the moment studying—categories run from "Riffle" through "Heavy" to "Not Recommended." Upset was a "Heavy" rapid, like Deubendorff. In the "Not Recommended" category there is only Lava Falls.

"Do you agree with that, Jerry?"

Sanderson grins with amusement, and speaks so slowly he seems wistful. "It's the granddaddy of them all," he says.

"There's a big drop, and a lot of boulders, and several holes like the one at Upset. You have to look the rapid over carefully, because the holes move."

In the stillness of a big eddy, the raft pauses under an overhanging cliff. Lava Falls fades in the conversation. Twenty-four miles is a lot of country. Through a cleft that reaches all the way down through the overhanging cliff a clear green stream is flowing into the river. The cleft is so narrow that the stream appears to be coming straight out of the sandstone. Actually, it meanders within the cliff and is thus lost to view. The water is so clear that it sends a pale-green shaft into the darker Colorado. The big river may no longer be red with silt, but it carries enough to remain opaque. In the small stream, the pebbles on the bottom are visible, magnified, distinct. "Dive in," Brower suggests. "See where it goes."

Brower and I went into the stream and into the cliff. The current was not powerful, coming through the rock, and the water was only four feet deep. I swam, by choice—the water felt so good. It felt cool, but it must have been about seventy-five degrees. It was cooler than the air. Within the cliff was deep twilight, and the echoing sound of the moving water. A bend to the right, a bend to the left, right, left—this stone labyrinth with a crystal stream in it was moment enough, no matter where it ended, but there lay beyond it a world that humbled the mind's eye. The walls widened first into a cascaded gorge and then flared out to become the ovate sides of a deep valley, into which the stream rose in tiers of pools and waterfalls. Some of the falls were only two feet high, others four feet, six feet. There were hundreds of them. The pools were as much as fifteen feet deep, and the water in them was white where it plunged and foamed, then blue in a wide circle around the plunge point, and pale green in the outer peripheries. This was Havasu Canyon, the immemorial home of the Havasupai, whose tribal name means "the people of the blue-green waters." We climbed from one pool to another, and swam across the pools, and let the waterfalls beat down around our shoulders. Mile after mile, the pools and waterfalls continued. The high walls of the valley were bright red. Nothing grew on these dry and flaky slopes from the mesa rim down about two-thirds of the way; then life began to show in isolated barrel cactus and prickly pear. The cacti thickened farther down, and below them was riverine vegetation—green groves of oak and cottonwood, willows and tamarisk, stands of cattail, tall grasses, moss, watercress, and maidenhair fern. The Havasupai have lived in this place for hundreds, possibly thousands, of years, and their population has remained stable. There are something like two hundred of them. They gather nuts on the canyon rim in winter and grow vegetables in the canyon in summer. They live about twelve miles up Havasu Creek from the Colorado. Moss covered the rocks around the blue-and-green pools. The moss on dry rock was soft and dense, and felt like broadloom underfoot. Moss also grew below the water's surface, where it was coated with travertine, and resembled coral. The stream was loaded with calcium, and this was the physical explanation of the great beauty of Havasu Canyon, for it was the travertine—crystalline calcium carbonate—that had both fashioned and secured the all but unending stairway of falls and pools. At the downstream lip of each plunge pool, calcium deposits had built up into natural dams, and these travertine dams were what kept Havasu Creek from running freely downhill. The dams were whitish tan, and so smooth and symmetrical that they might have been finished by a mason. They were two or three feet high. They sloped. Their crests were flat and smooth and with astonishing uniformity were about four inches thick from bank to bank. Brower looked up at the red canyon walls. He was sitting on the travertine, with one foot in a waterfall, and I was treading the green water below him. He said, "If Hualapai Dam had been built, or were ever built, this place where you are swimming would be at the bottom of a hundred feet of water." It was time to go back to the Colorado. I swam to the travertine dam at the foot of the pool, climbed up on it and dived into the pool below it, and swam across and dived again, and swam and dived—and so on for nearly two miles. Dominy was waiting below. "It's fabulous," he said. "I know every river canyon in the country, and this is the prettiest in the West."

▲

Mile 171. Beside the minor rapids at Gateway Canyon, we stop, unload the raft, and lay out our gear before settling

237

down to drinks before dinner. Brower is just beyond ear-shot. Dominy asks me again, "What did Dave do during the war?"

I tell him all I happen to know—that Brower trained troops in climbing techniques in West Virginia and Colorado, and that he later went with the 10th Mountain Division to Italy, where he won the Bronze Star.

Dominy contemplates the river. Brower goes to the water's edge and dips his Sierra Club cup. He will add whiskey to the water. "Fast-moving water is a very satisfying sound," Dominy says to him. "There is nothing more soothing than the sound of running or falling water."

"The river talks to itself, Floyd. Those little whirls, the sucks and the boils—they say things."

"I love to see white water, Dave. In all my trips through the West over the years, I have found moving streams with steep drops to them the most scenic things of all."

Over the drinks, Brower tells him, "I will come out of this trip different from when I came in. I am not in favor of dams, but I am in favor of Dominy. I can see what you have meant to the Bureau, and I am worried about what is going to happen there someday without you."

"No one will ever say that Dominy did not tell anyone and everyone exactly what he thinks, Dave."

"I've never heard anything different, Floyd."

"And, I might say, I've never heard anything different about you."

"I needed this trip more than anyone else."

"You're God-damned right you did, with that white skin."

238

Dominy takes his next drink out of the Sierra Club cup. The bottle of whiskey is nearly empty. Dominy goes far down into his briefcase and brings out another. It is Jim Beam. Dominy is fantastically loyal to Jim Beam. At his farm in Virginia a few weeks ago, he revived a sick calf by shooting it with a hypodermic syringe full of penicillin, condensed milk, and Jim Beam. Brower says he does not believe in penicillin.

"As a matter of fact, Dave Brower, I'll make a trip with you any time, anywhere."

"Great," Brower mutters faintly.

"Up to this point, Dave, we've won a few and lost a few —each of us. Each of us. Each of us. God damn it, everything Dave Brower does is O.K.—tonight. Dave, now that we've buried the hatchet, you've got to come out to my farm in the Shenandoah."

"Great."

To have a look at the map of the river, Dominy puts on Brower's glasses. Brower's glasses are No. 22s off the counter of F. W. Woolworth in San Francisco. Dominy rolls the scroll back to the Upset Rapid.

"How come you didn't go through there, Dave?"

"I'm chicken."

"Are you going to go through Lava Falls?"

"No."

"No?"

"No, thank you. I'll walk."

Upstream from where we sit, we can see about a mile of straight river between the high walls of the inner gorge, and

239

downstream this corridor leads on to a bold stone portal. Dominy contemplates the scene. He says, "With Hualapai Dam, you'd really have a lake of water down this far."

"Yes. A hundred and sixty feet deep," notes Brower.

"It would be beautiful, and, like Lake Powell, it would be better for *all* elements of society."

"There's another view, and I have it, and I suppose I'll die with it, Floyd. Lake Powell is a drag strip for power boats. It's for people who won't do things except the easy way. The magic of Glen Canyon is dead. It has been vulgarized. Putting water in the Cathedral in the Desert was like urinating in the crypt of St. Peter's. I hope it never happens here."

"Look, Dave. I don't live in a God-damned apartment. I didn't grow up in a God-damned city. Don't give me the crap that you're the only man that understands these things. I'm a greater conservationist than you are, by far. I do things. I make things available to man. Unregulated, the Colorado River wouldn't be worth a good God damn to anybody. You conservationists are phony outdoorsmen. I'm sick and tired of a democracy that's run by a noisy minority. I'm fed up clear to my God-damned gullet. I had the guts to come out and fight you bastards. You're just a bunch of phonies and you'll stoop to any kind of God-damned argument. That's why I took my pictures. You were misleading the public about what would happen here. You gave the impression that the whole canyon was going to be inundated by the reservoir. Your weapon is emotion. You guys are just not very God-damned honorable in your fights."

"I had hoped things would not take this turn, Floyd, but you're wrong."

"Do you want to keep this country the way it is for a handful of people?"

"Yes, I do. Hualapai Dam is not a necessity. You don't even want the water."

"We mainly want the power head, but the dam would be part of the over-all storage project under the Colorado Compact."

"The Colorado Compact was not found on a tablet written on Mount Sinai. Hualapai Dam is not necessary, and neither was Glen Canyon. Glen Canyon Dam was built for the greater good of Los Angeles."

"You're too intelligent to believe that."

"You're too intelligent not to believe that."

"For Christ's sake, be objective, Dave. Be reasonable."

"Some of my colleagues make the error of trying to be reasonable, Floyd. Objectivity is the greatest threat to the United States today."

▲

Mile 177, 9:45 A.M. The water is quite deep and serene here, backed up from the rapid. Lava Falls is two miles downstream, but we have long since entered its chamber of quiet.

"The calm before the storm," Brower says.

The walls of the canyon are black with lava—flows, cascades, and dikes of lava. Lava once poured into the canyon in this segment of the river. The river was here, much in its present form. It had long since excavated the canyon, for the volcanism occurred in relatively recent time. Lava came up through the riverbed, out from the canyon walls, and even down over the rims. It sent the Colorado up in clouds. It hardened, and it formed a dam and backed water two hundred miles.

"If a lava flow were to occur in the Grand Canyon today, Brower and the nature lovers would shout to high heaven that a great thing had happened," Dominy said, addressing everyone in the raft. "But if a man builds a dam to bring water and power to other men, it is called desecration. Am I right or wrong, Dave? Be honest."

"The lava dam of Quaternary time was eventually broken down by the river. This is what the Colorado will do to the Dominy dams that are in it now or are ever built. It will wipe them out, recover its grade, and go on about its business. But by then our civilization and several others will be long gone."

We drift past an enormous black megalith standing in the river. For eighty years, it was called the Niggerhead. It is the neck of a volcano, and it is now called Vulcan's Forge. We have a mile to go. Brower talks about the amazing size of the crystals on the canyon walls, the morning light in the canyon, the high palisades of columnar basalt. No one else says much of anything. All jokes have been cracked twice. We are just waiting, and the first thing we hear is the sound. It is a big, tympanic sound that increasingly fills the canyon. The water around us is dark-green glass. Five hundred yards. There it is. Lava Falls. It is, of course, a rapid, not a waterfall. There is no smooth lip. What we now see ahead of us at this distance appears to be a low whitewashed wall.

The raft touches the riverbank. Sanderson gets out to inspect the rapid, and we go, too. We stand on a black ledge, in the roar of the torrent, and look at the water. It goes everywhere. From bank to bank, the river is filled with boulders, and the water smashes into them, sends up auroras of spray, curls thickly, and pounds straight down into bomb-crater holes. It eddies into pockets of lethal calm and it doubles back to hit itself. Its valleys are deeper and its hills are higher than in any other rapid in North America. The drop is prodigious—twenty-six feet in a hundred yards—but that is only half the story. Prospect Creek, rising black-walled like a coal chute across the river, has shoved enough rock in here to stop six rivers, and this has produced the preëminent rapid of the Colorado.

When Dominy stepped up on the ledge and into the immediacy of Lava Falls, he shouted above the thunder, "Boy, that's a son of a bitch! Look at those *rocks!* See that hole over there? Jesus! Look at that one!"

Brower said, "Look at the way the water swirls. It's alive!"

The phys.-ed. teacher said, "Boy, that could tear the hell out of your bod."

Brower said, "Few come, but thousands drown."

243

Dominy said, "If I were Jerry, I'd go to the left and then try to move to the right."

Lava protruded from the banks in jagged masses, particularly on the right, and there was a boulder there that looked like an axe blade. Brower said, "I'd go in on the right and out on the left."

My own view was that the river would make all the decisions. I asked Sanderson how he planned to approach what we saw there.

"There's only one way to do it," he said. "We go to the right."

The raft moved into the river slowly, and turned, and moved toward the low white wall. A hundred yards. Seventy-five yards. Fifty yards. It seems odd, but I did not notice until just then that Brower was on the raft. He was, in fact, beside me. His legs were braced, his hands were tight on a safety rope, and his Sierra Club cup was hooked in his belt. The tendons in his neck were taut. His chin was up. His eyes looked straight down the river. From a shirt pocket Dominy withdrew a cigar. He lighted it and took a voluminous drag. We had remaining about fifteen seconds of calm water. He said, "I might bite an inch off the end, but I doubt it." Then we went into Lava Falls.

Water welled up like a cushion against the big boulder on the right, and the raft went straight into it, but the pillow of crashing water was so thick that it acted on the raft like a great rubber fender between a wharf and a ship. We slid off the rock and to the left—into the craterscape. The raft bent like a V, flipped open, and shuddered forward. The little outboard—it represented all the choice we had—cavitated, and screamed in the air. Water rose up in tons through the bottom of the raft. It came in from the left, the right, and above. It felt great. It covered us, pounded us, lifted us, and heaved us scudding to the base of the rapid.

For a moment, we sat quietly in the calm, looking back. Then Brower said, "The foot of Lava Falls would be two hundred and twenty-five feet beneath the surface of Lake Dominy."

Dominy said nothing. He just sat there, drawing on a wet, dead cigar. Ten minutes later, however, in the dry and baking Arizona air, he struck a match and lighted the cigar again.